After Her Brain Broke

After Her Brain Broke

Helping My Daughter Recover Her Sanity

Susan Inman

Bridgeross Communications, Dundas, Ontario, Canada

Library and Archives Canada Cataloguing in Publication

Inman, Susan, 1949-
    After her brain broke : helping my daughter recover her sanity /
Susan
Inman ; with an introduction by Michael Kirby.

Includes bibliographical references.
ISBN 978-0-9810037-8-8

    1. Inman, Molly--Mental health. 2. Inman, Susan, 1949-. 3.
Schizophrenia
in children--Patients--British Columbia--Vancouver--Biography. 4.
Parents
of mentally ill children--British Columbia--Vancouver--Biography.
5. Mothers and daughters--British Columbia--Vancouver--Biography. I.
Title.

RJ506.S3I56 2010   616.89'80092   C2010-900552-
X

First Published in 2010 by Bridgeross Communications,
Dundas, Ontario, Canada

Universal Praise for this Book

E. Fuller Torrey, MD, Bestselling author of *Surviving Schizophrenia*, Executive Director, The Stanley Medical Research Foundation, founding director, The Treatment Advocacy Centre, former advisor, the National Alliance for the Mentally Ill (NAMI), Bethesda, MD, USA

Susan Inman's book is one of the best accounts I have read of serious mental illness as told by a mother. Very nicely written, she describes the occasional highlights and more common lowlights of the psychiatric care system, as experienced by her daughter. Ms. Inman's attempts to educate herself and her support of her daughter as they wend their way through the schizoaffective therapeutic maze provide a model for other families. Highly recommended.

Daniel Kalla, MD, International Bestselling Author of *Pandemic, Rage Therapy, Blood Lies*, and *Of Flesh And Blood* and Emergency Room Physician, St Paul's Hospital, Vancouver

A harrowing, heart-wrenching, and ultimately triumphant story of one family's struggle with a child's mental illness. It's impossible not to be moved by Susan Inman's honest and touching account of her daughter's sudden descent into mental health turmoil and the family's long hard battle to overcome it. A must read for families coping with a mental illness, and a wonderful eye-opener for those of us lucky enough not to have been affected.

Stephanie Engel, MD, Psychiatrist, Harvard University

Susan Inman has written a much needed book about her experience as a mother coming to grips with her daughter's devastating mental illness. Other parents will recognize and take comfort from her courageous and persistent efforts to learn what is known about psychotic illnesses and their treatment, while holding tenaciously to her own personal knowledge of what it means to be a loving, humane and thoughtful parent. Believing in one's own instincts as a parent in the face of expertise, myths and prejudices is a monumental task, and Ms Inman does it with grace and conviction.

Jehannine C. Austin, PhD, Assistant Professor, Departments of Psychiatry and Medical Genetics, University of British Columbia

Susan Inman eloquently and movingly describes her journey through her daughter's illness. She illuminates the often neglected struggles of people whose family members have serious mental illness. Her powerful story offers hope and validation to others who find themselves in similar situations.

Without self-pity, Inman shares experiences that amount to systematic vilification by the mental health system. For those of us working within it, this induces a sick shudder of recognition. Yet, it also provides an opportunity to reflect upon how we perceive and interact with family members of those with serious mental illness. Inman has produced a book that constitutes important reading for both family members and mental health professionals alike.

P. Jane Milliken, RN, PhD, Associate Professor, School of Nursing, University of Victoria, British Columbia

Susan Inman's story mirrors that of other parents and family members who love and care for a mentally ill relative. Anguish, frustration, sadness, and the inability to know how to act and react can define their lives. Susan's story is inspirational because she also models the sheer determination, resourcefulness, and personal strength that can develop when steering a loved one toward recovery, through a world still plagued by misunderstanding and intolerance, rather than empathy and compassion.

Renea Mohammed, Program Coordinator, Vancouver Community Mental Health Services Peer Support Program

This is an important and powerful work that not only illustrates what it is like for families touched by mental illness, but also serves as a reminder of the tremendous resource that family can be for those of us recovering from a mental health issue. Family members are, for many of us, the ones who will go that extra mile. They are the unsung heroes in many a story. Susan's book demonstrates very aptly the difference that family can make and the importance of having a mental health system that works with them.

To MJS
whose spirit endures

For
Peter and Naomi
who sustain me
and
for all the countless families
who are launched on this unexpected journey

Acknowledgements

Noah Seixas, who came when we needed him

Kitty and Michael, Gloria and Bob and Ben, Susan and Steve, Heather and John, Ann and Jack, Joan, Linda and Kris, Kim, Penny, Barbara, Ann, Marge, Sandra, Caroline, Starla, Muriel, Sue, Rita and Chris, Eufemia, the Patricias, Donna, Dominica, Deirdre, Pat, Vicki and Pat, Terry and Tammy, Teri, Holly, Lembi, Carmen, Glida, Sharon, Wendy, Sherry, Cindy, Allison, Joanne, Marguerite and Herschel, Maria, Sherry, Jane, Phillip, Lyn, Mark, Eleanor, Marilyn, Dick, Esther, Ellen, and many others who shared their difficult stories with me

Annick Aubert, who came to CAMH to tell me about the Toronto families and then led me to June Conway-Beeby who led me to Marvin Ross

Kim Calsaferri, Shirley Rogers, and Sri Pendakur of Vancouver Coastal Mental Health Services

Rosa, Kadriye, Naim, Roland, Susan, Regina, Rosie, Natalie and Sheana who haven't forgotten her

Howard Chodos, a masterful facilitator of communication, who showed this book to Michael and Ella

NAMI – Greater Seattle, who connected me to Seth Dawson's e-list which lets me see what a professional advocate can accomplish

Joyce Burland of NAMI who keeps showing families that knowledge is power

Sally Cohen Haskell, my supportive sister

Dr. Debbie Thompson, a brilliant psychopharmacologist who is generous with her knowledge

Susan Hirschman, who, during a brisk walk on a chilly Manhattan evening, told me I had a dramatic story to tell

And always to Peter Seixas, who knew this was possible before I did

Table of Contents

Introduction

Mental Health Commission of Canada

Susan Inman's account provides glimpses of the heartache and devastation a family experiences when mental illness strikes. In a measured tone devoid of drama or embellishment, she describes her travail over the nine years of her daughter's illness, a "devoted and desperate" mother.

Recognizing that the progression of mental illness can be a puzzling, unsettling, and long-term experience, she is frustrated at the lack of sensitivity and compassion many healthcare professionals demonstrate. It is only when she encounters kind and caring ones that she realizes how different the experience can be.

While critical of the guidance and help professionals should – but often don't – provide to families, Susan is even harsher with herself and often wonders if she had done everything she could for her daughter (" ...was there some way that I could have gotten this prescription in the previous year that I didn't consider?").

One wonders if Susan's daughter, Molly, is doing better today because of or in spite of some of the professional advice she has received over the years. What is clear is that Susan is resolute and unwavering in her determination to help Molly. Most families wish to demonstrate the same integrity, but many don't have the inner strength – or the proper support – to carry on. Mental illness wreaks havoc on the entire family.

Susan's heart-wrenching account is an important reminder of the work we still have to do to ensure that people with mental illness and their families get the same treatment and respect that individuals with physical illnesses receive. It is also testimony to the devotion and dedication of families, which sadly often comes at the expense of their own well-being.

Michael Kirby
Chair

Ella Amir, Chair, Family
Caregivers' Advisory
Committee

Down the Stairs

May 1ˢᵗ, 2000

Molly stomps down the stairs, raging, but we are not sure about what.

"We're so happy to see you," we say, trying to take in the unfamiliar person in front of us. "We're glad to be home."

She wildly scans the living room. "I hate Aleyan. I hate, hate Aleyan."

What's been going on here? Aleyan is our cherished neighbour, Molly's special friend from infancy, and her phone calls about Molly's increasingly strange behaviour during our week away have been frightening. Molly hasn't wanted to talk to us. We attribute this unusual lack of interest in the phone calls to her new, very assertive stance. Finally, at fifteen, she has seemed eager to separate. She must have needed all of this therapy and the new anti-depressants that have helped her continue to go to school. School's become such an ordeal. How could we have missed these terrible learning disabilities that the private educational psychologist we've hired has recently told us about?

"What did Aleyan do?"

Molly glares with suspicion. "She doesn't listen. She doesn't respect me."

"That's terrible. What wasn't she listening about?"

The question stumps her and she bolts upstairs.

She hurls her words back down. "You never listen to me! This family is dysfunctional! It's full of secrets and lies!"

We are speechless. Where are these words and these ideas coming from? Molly has always been very warmly connected to her family but painfully shy with her peers. What exactly has been happening with Molly's therapist? She's never wanted to meet with us. We've accepted her explanation that Molly wishes to keep her sessions with her private. This sounds like a harmless request, especially because we've been eager to support any evidence of Molly's urges for independence. We've come to think of these sessions like Molly's now necessary visits to her very supportive and skilful math tutor. Something that could make this extremely rocky transition to adolescence and the demands of school go better.

"Do you want to sit down and tell us what you're thinking?" We settle in the comfy living room, our smiles urging her to join us. "What lie have we told you?"

"Stand up! I didn't say you could sit down. You didn't ask me if that was okay!" I can barely recognize her voice.

What has she been discussing with Veronica, the therapist? Or Veronica with her? We've been looking for clues about the actual content of these sessions. Is there something that we really ought to know about besides the bullying incidents at school that caused her great distress? When we try to ask Veronica, she vaguely alludes to more dimensions of the bullying than we'd understood. These incidents seemed upsetting enough that we'd found our way to Veronica's office. We were sure that skills training in assertiveness with a counselling psychologist could help her develop the playground smarts that have always been hard for her.

"Is this a good place to stand?" we ask, positioning ourselves at the foot of the stairs.

She's pacing on the landing, repeating her complaints as she pounds her feet, faster and faster, trapped in some arrhythmic dance that's possessed her. In the deep lurches of my childhood mind, I know I've seen these behaviours.

"Tell us more about what's upset you?"

"Don't talk to me!" she yells as she talks more and more to herself. "This is shit! Total shit! You can't treat me like this."

We go into the kitchen to whisper. Peter will call Dr. A, our family physician, for an emergency appointment. This must relate to the Paxil.

The new-found energy Molly had developed with 10 mg of Paxil had grown larger with 20 mg. I had been sitting in Dr. A's waiting room during these appointments, confidently respecting and encouraging Molly's privacy. When Molly emerged with the prescription for 30 mg, I'd rushed to get Dr. A's attention. I wanted her to know that Molly seemed somewhat overwhelmed by the 20 mg, and to convey to her that it was as if Molly was not sure what to do with this newly arrived but somewhat volatile energy.

With a sharp look conveying her impatience at my lack of awareness of my own daughter, Dr. A told me that Molly's depression hadn't lifted. She turned away and we went to fill the prescription. When we returned in two weeks, I tried to tell her about Molly's increased anger. I wished she could understand that we are the kind of parents who expect teenage anger. Our older daughter, Naomi, was furious at sixteen when we vetoed her car trip to California with friends. But we can't find any issues as Molly's new found temper flares up.

Earlier this spring, Dr. A had handed me a prescription for 40 mg of Paxil which I'd learned from computer searches is a hefty dose. Molly is tiny. "I'd like to just get a renewal for 30 mg capsules," I had said, in my friendly but firm voice, hoping to remind her that she'd launched these medications at our request when we met with her to discuss our worries about Molly's growing depression.

"This is the prescription you need to fill."

The coldness shocked me. Other patients in the waiting room were beginning to watch. I took the prescription and prepared an odd but eventually effective plan as we left. I phoned Peter who was also troubled to hear her response, and he dutifully called her from his office at The University of British Columbia (UBC). He explained, with more compelling details, why we didn't want to raise Molly's dosage. Sure enough, a professor trumped a mother, and Dr. A backed down. She phoned the pharmacy to renew the 30 mg dose.

Molly has begun shouting at us again. "This family is full of secrets and lies! Secrets and lies! Secrets and lies." It sounds like Dr. Phil except Molly doesn't watch these types of shows and never uses any kind of language like this. The words seem to focus her as if she's explaining to herself the torrents of raging energy fuelling her.

"What secret is there, sweetie?"

16

Molly has always loved affectionate names but I shouldn't have said this. Trying to be affectionate and reasonable isn't working.

She rushes down the stairs just as Peter rejoins me.

"I hate you both! Look what you've done to me!"

I back away as Peter begins cajoling her into the car. We are suddenly learning new skills. Our kids kept being cooperative as they grew up. Especially Molly, whose unusual need to stay close to us we attributed to her own unique developmental plan. We have great faith in our child-rearing philosophies. Peter's is based on observing the practices of his parents whose expertise in nurturing created very confident and productive children. My ideas spring from a relentless examination of child-rearing literature.

Together we believe that our sensitive affirmation of our children and their evolving needs is all that is required. We assume that our understanding of the growth and development of children is pretty evolved and that it will lead to predictable results. Or at least we did before we had our fifteen-year-old daughter, who is looking increasingly bizarre, pounding her fists into the backseat of the car muttering in furious bursts of swear words she's never needed to use before.

Dr. A has agreed to the emergency appointment. Trying to walk with Molly into her office is almost impossible. She careens away, heading off in random directions, only gradually arriving at the waiting room door from where we watch her. The connection between us, always so solid, is vanishing.

There are lots of empty seats in the waiting room which is good since Molly can't settle, selecting one after another, each quickly proving itself to be unacceptable. I see the receptionist pick up the phone and Dr. A emerges, warmly inviting us all into the largest of the consulting rooms. No chair looks right here and Molly fidgets by the door.

Dr. A focuses on Molly. "How is the Paxil doing?"

Molly's face searches the room for an answer just before she steps forward and kicks Dr. A's desk.

"Do you think the dose is right?" Dr. A asks. "What dose would you like to be on?"

Peter and I look at each other. What have we done? How could we have gotten ourselves and Molly into such an impossible situation. We try to take over.

"We think something's really wrong. Molly's never been like this."

By now she's hunched in a corner sputtering with rage. "Maybe she should see a psychiatrist?"

"I could make you a referral," Dr. A offers, sounding relieved that she knows what to do. She pauses, "But it takes months to see someone."

Does she think we should try to get Molly home and wait for the appointment?

"Of course, sometimes if you arrive at emergency at Children's Hospital, you can get assigned a psychiatrist."

A plan! We know how to follow through on plans. If there's a way to get connected to a psychiatrist at Children's, we will find it.

Molly initially seems calmed by the sights and sounds of Children's Hospital. Maybe she associates it with solving the rare health problems that have brought her here before. But the waits have never been this long before. And the waiting room isn't really that busy. We've explained the situation to the triage nurse but somehow Molly's condition must be less serious than that of the other children who are resting in their parents' arms or playing with the stacking toys in the corner. Molly has become fascinated by a toddler. And found a ball to roll to him. Her heightened animation has captured the little boy's attention. She actually looks quite cheerful.

After what seems like hours, a young woman who must be a resident calls for Molly. In less than five minutes she asks us in. "I've been explaining to Molly about how moods work."

Moods? What term is this?

She's drawn a line across the middle of a piece of notepaper. "This end is when we feel really sad, like Molly had felt. And this end is when we feel extremely happy but with no real reason, like Molly is feeling now." Molly's face has settled into a slightly eerie grin as she nods knowingly at us or at something. "But, I've been explaining to Molly that people usually operate in the middle."

Okay. Where is this going?

"Does anyone in either of your families have bipolar disorder?"

Peter says no and I start to agree and then one of the biggest realizations of my life hits me. How could I have not known until now? After the years of studying psychology and the years of therapy to explain my chaotic childhood. "I... think... my mother might have had bipolar disorder, but it was never diagnosed."

"Okay, well that might be what we're looking at. We have a unit here, CAPE, where Molly could stay for a week and we could assess her. "

Molly is eager to go someplace new. Suddenly she's on a great adventure. And so are we, but we're not feeling so great about it.

Children's Hospital

May, June, and July 2000

Molly's surprisingly cooperative as we help settle her into her room. Until she realizes that the whole unit is locked. "I won't stay here! You can't make me!"

We distract her with introductions to the friendly-looking staff. She's become very gregarious by the time we leave with a long list of things for the suitcase I'll return with in an hour. Later, I find her on a couch in the common area, the TV show not really attracting any of the kids who buzz around the room in various states of mental and physical disarray. She lets me set-up her room with her favourite quilt and best pillow. She looks young and lost.

The plan, we learn the next day, is to take her off the Paxil over the week. After a few days, one of the nurses seems to trust us enough, from our twice daily visits, to say that the unit gets lots of "Paxil kids" all the time. Dr. B, the head of the unit, doesn't mention this when she meets with us to get background information.

We desperately want her to take Molly on as a patient and, eventually, she accepts Molly's case into what is obviously an overwhelming load. She wants to hear anything that can help her establish Molly's baseline and understand what has been happening. We give her Veronica's phone number in case Molly, as Veronica has vaguely suggested, has actually recounted something that we don't know about. Later, I'll add this piece of

21

thoroughness on my part to the list of mistakes that I make along the way.

It's possible, Dr. B tells us, that as the Paxil leaves her system, Molly will just return to normal. I worry that these terrifying days will trouble her, but Dr. B suggests that if she gets better, she'll just gradually forget about this experience. However, she also suggests that we put her name on the waiting list for C1, the long-term assessment unit, in case she needs more care.

We agree to this but already see Molly beginning to return to normal and don't think we'll need this much sought-after bed. We aren't actually the kind of people whose kids have really big problems. It's too bad that some parents aren't able to take good care of their children; we've been lucky in that we've had time to raise our daughters with the sensitive, loving energy all children need. If only more people realized how important it is to carefully meet their children's needs when they are young so that they can secure them a solid foundation for the future.

Naomi, our elder daughter, flies home the third day. The term has ended at McGill University in Montreal and she wants to help. She's in time for the evening visit to Molly. We've brought our Scrabble game and Molly is focusing better and having fun as we joke our way through the evening. Patients are only supposed to have two visitors, but the staff is flexible and supportive. Being all together feels right. In the silence underneath the laughing, we are reminding ourselves that we know how to take care of each other. Our family has been thrown into this traumatic experience but we've gotten through it. It will be over soon.

When we arrive with Boggle the next afternoon, the head nurse looks embarrassed. Her voice sounds professional and insistent, "I can't let you all be here. Patients are only allowed two guests. One of you will have to leave."

We reorganize our plans in the hall outside the unit and Naomi leaves. The nurse appears, motioning me aside. "I'm sorry about this. You might want to know that the therapist told the psychiatrist that your family is dysfunctional, and you shouldn't all be around Molly too much."

The words knock my breath out. Why would Veronica say such a thing? After three years, she's only referred to the bullying problem at school when we try to talk with her. I wonder if the call from the hospital forces her to say something about what's been happening for three years, and she's felt forced to come up with this. Doesn't she know how destructive such an offhand comment could be? And doesn't she realize how untrue her "assessment" is? What exactly does she mean by dysfunctional? It's time to call her and ask for a meeting.

Veronica is her bubbly self on the phone. I've watched her in the three years that Peter and I have alternated driving Molly to her office which is an hour away from our house. I'm not pleased with some of the brief interactions I get to have with her before and after the appointments. Although I'm eager to establish a rapport with her, her attempts to build a relationship seem disingenuous. She's let me know she's a jogger, and, in a confidential tone, tells me how sad it is that some people run for the wrong reasons.

I'm not sure what to make of her and her invitation to forge our relationship based on our ability to know better than "some people." However, after long days of teaching, the wait for Molly in the empty seating area gives me a chance to have the nap I usually crave. I awake refreshed, ready for the rush hour drive home to make the dinner which will reunite our family. These dinners help prepare us for the evening ahead. Peter's had to become an increasingly involved tutor for Molly and I need the time for lesson planning.

Before discussing with Veronica the comments she's made to the psychiatrist, I explain to her that Molly might have bipolar disorder. She jumps in to reassure me that she's unusually well-equipped to deal with bipolar disorders. Her niece has bipolar disorder and she's been very involved in helping her become stable. This is good news and I ask about what I should read; I'm on my way to the bookstore and will be checking on Amazon.

In her confidential tone, she tells me that there's only one book I need and only one book that I should read: Kay Jamieson's *An Unquiet Mind*. I prickle at the notion that anyone would think there's only one useful book; surely there must be more material available since I've now been told that 1 in 100 people has bipolar disorder.

I don't challenge her judgement because I want to ask her instead about the comment labelling our family as dysfunctional. There's a pause and I sense her scrambling to explain. She bounces back with the explanation, again in her manner of confiding something important that affirms our special understanding; the resident with whom she spoke was obviously very young; she didn't catch what Veronica meant.

Okay, but what did Veronica mean and, if she actually believes something doesn't seem right in our family, what exactly is she thinking is the problem? She'll talk with us more when we make an appointment after Molly is released.

Dr. Kay Jamieson's memoir details her disintegration, while teaching at UCLA's Department of Psychology, into the frenzy of a manic psychosis. It's riveting and especially poignant since all the campus landmarks she describes are very familiar to me from my own graduate school days at UCLA's Department of Dance.

I learn a lot about bipolar disorder, lots of things I hadn't learned during my training in dance therapy at UCLA. During these years in this program, psychiatric diagnoses were understood to get in the way of engaging the patient in the growth-producing events our work was supposed to bring them. Kay Jamieson's brilliance shines on every page and, although I am heartened for Molly to share a diagnosis with such a star, I don't think I am really getting the full picture of this complicated disorder.

We're all relieved when Molly is released. She's unsteady but maybe the Paxil hasn't completely left her brain. She still is uncharacteristically feisty. She calls one of her few friends, a girl on Saturna Island, whose mother has recently been diagnosed with breast cancer. She arranges to go to visit her in a week. She still doesn't seem stable enough to go back to school and this trip requires two ferry rides and staying at a household which is profoundly stressed. Molly's usually quite thoughtful about people's problems, but she is oblivious about imposing on this wounded family and annoyed that we are interfering.

We finally have an appointment with Veronica. Soon after the four of us and Veronica settle into her spacious and carefully designed office, we hear a whimper. Nate, her black lab who is always present and apparently key to some of her therapeutic strategies, is vomiting. She's very gentle with Nate and we wait while she cleans up and comforts him, aware that the clock is ticking and other patients will be waiting. We never let ourselves question, at this point, the benefits of the $10,000 we have spent on these $110-an-hour sessions. It's all worth it to help Molly grow safely into her next stages.

Veronica returns with a focused expression. But I'm soon frustrated. The focus isn't about our situation; she's mulling over another family that's been in distress. She speaks slowly, maybe intentionally building a kind of suspense. She uses her confiding tone to share with us a story about how much trouble this family had been having. We sense that we should rejoice with her that the family is doing well now that the mother's alcoholism has been ferreted out by Veronica and that she's in treatment. She smiles patiently, waiting.

None of us is clear about why she lets herself be distracted by this irrelevant story at this point and Peter and I try to guide her back to our concerns. Molly, not yet well enough to return to school, wants to go for the weekend to visit a friend on Saturna Island. Finally, the adults will be able to join forces and help establish a reasonable framework from which to deal with this inappropriate plan.

Veronica turns to Molly, beaming her broad smile, "Oh, Molly. Saturna is such a beautiful place to be. How wonderful that you've been able to plan this all by yourself!"

Peter and I are dumbfounded. Naomi flashes us a vindicated look. Since her return she's worked her endless contacts and has reported back to us that many people see Veronica as flakey. Flakey? But she has stature in the community.

We don't know what to say but Veronica seems to be on a roll. She and Nate will be going to her Mayne Island house on the weekend and she'll arrange to be with Molly until she gets off the ferry; Molly can somehow then continue on to Saturna and get to her friend's house. Molly melts in this display of thoughtfulness and turns on us, "And you didn't even want me to go! And her mother has breast cancer and you wanted to keep me away!" We know we can't begin to sort out with her the skewed configuration of ideas that's developing.

We need to begin separating Molly from this ignorant and dangerous woman. How could we have ended up in this situation? When we wanted Molly to get additional support, Peter went to his colleagues in UBC's Faculty of Education.

As a historian, he didn't have much contact with students who'd completed MAs in the Counselling Psychology program. One colleague suggested Veronica, who'd been building a high profile reputation for herself. At this point, it hadn't concerned us that the graduates of this program weren't required to take a course on serious mental illnesses and that, even if they wanted to, this kind of basic course didn't, and still doesn't, exist in the program. I've learned more since then about the damage many poorly trained mental health professionals can do, but we were just getting our bearings as we sat in Veronica's office.

I begin telling Veronica how Dr. B will be seeing Molly in case this episode does develop into full blown bipolar disorder. I'm starting to create a plan in which Veronica can soon be phased out of the picture despite Molly's growing feeling that only Veronica understands her.

Before I can start to describe how lucky we are to have such an experienced psychiatrist willing to work with Molly, Veronica begins to explain her ideas about psychiatrists.

"Molly, you need to know that psychiatrists like to play mind games. It's just something they do. You have to be very careful not to get caught up in their stuff. You might need medication from Dr. B, but I'm still your therapist."

Molly looks reassured but the rest of us are sitting in stunned silence. The only person who has something to say is Veronica. "Naomi, I'd love to get a chance to get to know you better. Are you free tomorrow afternoon?"

The next day Naomi returns home from her session with Veronica exasperated with us. How could we have let this go on for so long? Veronica spent the hour with Naomi trying to find out more about "this strange relationship your mom has with your sister." Naomi let her know she didn't think there was anything strange at all in the relationship but that her painfully shy sister has never had an easy time making friends. Veronica didn't seem to think Naomi needed a follow-up appointment.

Peter, however, feels forced to arrange to take an insistent Molly to Saturna and stay with friends of friends while Molly makes the trip that Veronica had deemed necessary. Maybe because we'd explained we wouldn't be paying for Veronica's help with the trip, or she'd lost interest, she didn't seem concerned that we'd made other plans. Maybe she felt she'd done her work by demonstrating the way that supportive parents would respond to Molly's plans. Molly comes home even more shaken, confused by a party where people kept coming and going and she wasn't sure where she belonged. At least she is very willing to return with Peter.

Molly isn't in any shape to go back to school on Monday. The unpaid leave I'd arranged to take for the spring has been a great idea; I can stay with her as we wait for her to get over this rough time. Peter and I relax in the kitchen trying to figure out our next steps when Molly bolts into the room, very excited.

Usually dressed in nondescript jeans and sweatshirt, she's dressed herself up in her best outfit and lavishly applied some make-up. Before we can begin to discuss whether returning to classes is a reasonable idea, she races to the front door and triumphantly shouts goodbye as she slams it closed.

We decide that Peter should catch up with her and persuade her to wait longer before trying school again. He finds her at the bus stop and is met with a fury of criticism for trying to stop her. As the bus arrives, she charges to the door, forcefully shaking off Peter's hand on her arm as he tries to hold on to her.

The staff at University Hill Secondary School know she's been in Children's Hospital; they'd already been planning to meet to discuss her alternating angry and weepy behaviour before she was admitted.

Although we want to believe that maybe she could make it through a school day since she is suddenly very determined, we know she is still unstable. We leave a message for her counsellor to call us when Molly arrives. The counsellor calls to apologize; Molly had arrived at school but when she'd gone to check on her, no one could find her. Maybe we should come in and update the school.

By the time we arrive, the school constable is waiting for us. We are going to have help locating our missing daughter. The constable wonders if she has favourite places near the school. All we can think of is how Molly had begun running so slowly that she'd been getting lost in her PE class during their route through the forest.

What about her friends at school? She hasn't really made any friends at U Hill when she'd transferred to take the detested learning assistance classes she'd begun to need. The principal comes in; they've located Molly. She'd gone to her old school, PW, walked up to the office counter and demanded that they get her friend Katie out of class to talk to her. A counsellor, who knew her and could see something was very wrong, had guided her into his office. Somehow, when he'd called Katie into his office, both girls had ended up leaving the school.

We call Dr. B who tells us she can get Molly into the assessment unit; we should bring her in as soon as possible. Good idea. But where is she? When we try Katie's home number, she answers in a shaken voice. Is Molly with her? Can we talk to Molly?

"I don't know what to do," Katie is crying. "She's mad at you and doesn't want to live with you anymore."

We ask her to try to keep Molly with her while we drive over.

Molly's careful arrangement with her hair has begun falling out of its elastic and the mascara is smeared over her cheek. She isn't sure where her backpack is. She is sure though that she will now be living with Katie. We tell her that Dr. B really wants to talk with her; can she come with us to see her? She smirks at our stupidity; we are trying to trick her into going back to the hospital. "It was terrible, Katie. The door was locked! Look what they're trying to do to me! I'll never go back there."

How will we get her into the car this time? We call the helpful school constable and describe the situation. Molly gets on the phone explaining why she'll never go back to the hospital. As soon as the resourceful constable says she'll have to take her in a police car, she relents. She'll come as long as Katie comes, too.

This time the nurses at Children's Hospital are waiting for us but, still, we need to sit while paperwork is finished and staff at C1 get set-up. Katie keeps talking quietly with Molly who sits in a slump, sad and defeated. I want the two very tall security guards who've begun hanging around nearby to realize that there is a sensitive situation occurring and their presence will be intimidating to a shattered girl. I repeatedly try to catch their eye to clue them in to what is happening; they can wait somewhere else for whatever they are doing. They ignore me.

Dr. B appears but before she talks with us, she speaks to the guards and then they all approach us together. Molly begins screaming at the sight of them and I realize my body is shaking as I turn my mentally ill daughter over to people who are terrifying to her. How ridiculously naive I am; the imposing guards are here to make sure that Molly gets to the ward. Dr. B wants us to leave.

The early afternoon air is calm and empty as we walk back to the car.

When we visit the following day, Vancouver Children's Hospital's newly decorated lounges in the children's psychiatric unit inspire confidence. Cozy couches and chairs invite healing conversations in the open, airy space. I'm hoping that soon Molly will be having these kinds of conversations with us but she's been furious with us since her admission.

We've put her in a prison; why do we have the right to do this? The attempts at explanation about psychiatrists having certified her because she could be a danger to herself and because she needs treatment don't appease her. She seems to need and enjoy the twice daily rejections of me after I deliver her special requests for food to replace the hospital's meals. They do give her some sense of power in an environment where she doesn't feel she has any.

Somewhere in her muddled mind, I want her to hold on to the thought that we aren't abandoning her. I want her to understand that the rages that fuel her might be part of the illness that Dr. B has begun to treat. The Valproate Acid sounds like a good first choice. I've begun to read about medications and marvel that a substance that has been treating epilepsy for years, including our niece's epilepsy, now has an additional use. We expect Molly to return to herself soon.

Molly's anger does become less intense as the weeks pass by. She doesn't actively fight against the new firm diagnosis of bipolar disorder but neither does she actually acknowledge it and what it might mean in her life.

I become more concerned about the impact of the hospital on her. Though hostile to the staff, she's adjusted to the behaviour modification system that structures the days. Cooperative behaviour leads to more breaks outside. When I arrive for the afternoon food drop-offs, I begin to see her having her break with two of the tough looking girls from her unit who, I know, live in foster care.

These aren't the kinds of girls Molly's ever been attracted to previously which shouldn't be a problem except I see them smoking. For the last couple of years, one of Molly's pet peeves has been smoking and the evils of the tobacco industry. I wonder how long this attitude will last as these breaks with other angry girls continue. I find a nurse and explain the problem. Maybe Molly could have her breaks at different times to minimize the influence of these clearly troubled girls on her? It doesn't take very long to become addicted to cigarettes.

The nurse takes a deep breath before she begins her therapeutic work with me. I need to understand that Molly is now fifteen; I need to let go and allow her to grow up. She needs to be allowed to make her own decisions about whether she wants to become a smoker. I don't know what to say; she won't want to hear that encouraging independence is something we have always thoroughly valued and supported.

She must think that we have been sabotaging Molly's growth and now she's wisely noticed a teachable moment by catching me in the act of undermining her independence. I decide not to mention that Molly has been legally committed to a psychiatric facility because experts feel she isn't in her right mind to make major decisions for herself.

We are asked to attend a meeting with Dr. B and a social worker. I am not sure what a social worker will be able to offer us but we certainly could use some help in case Veronica remains a problem. But the meeting isn't about asking us what kind of help we might need in managing this new, confusing illness.

The social worker is present because Molly has reported that she was physically abused by Peter. She keeps telling people about how he grabbed her arm as she tried to run onto the bus. I know from teaching in schools that reports of abuse automatically lead to serious investigations so here we are. Molly has no other episodes of abuse to report.

The staff might wonder if this is because she is still suspicious of them or the abuse is too traumatic to confront. Perhaps they know enough to wonder if this "abuse" was the desperate attempt of a father trying to hold on to his manic daughter as she raced into a world she could no longer understand.

I look at the social worker's face and hope for the best. She appears to be a no-nonsense middle-aged woman with discerning eyes. I try to explain that we are novices in dealing with genuinely difficult behaviour from our children. Our discipline skills have been limited to sending Naomi to her room several times, as a preschooler, to think about some transgression we can no longer remember.

Molly never needed this kind of punishment. I'd never considered her "terrible two" tantrums as misbehaviour. One expert in a book had recommended a strategy that made sense. I would just stay nearby, quietly witnessing her flailing and letting her know that I was sorry she was feeling so bad.

When she'd regained control, she always yearned to be held and comforted. This approach worked and the period of these tantrums disappeared. Our kids kept making themselves easy to raise and helped us feel that we knew or could learn all the right things to do. But now nothing is working.

I want the social worker to understand that we need help in dealing with the behaviours we are now seeing. The social worker doesn't have any suggestions but she must have realized there wasn't any abuse to investigate because we never see her again. I later realize how lucky we were. Only a third of UBC's undergraduate social work students take the program's one elective course on serious mental illnesses. This woman must have been able to learn on the job.

After six weeks, I'm relieved that Molly hasn't become a smoker. She has, however, heard from her new friends about group homes. A couple of the teens are already in group homes and brag about their cool escapades. Molly thinks a group home will be the best option for her since her parents don't understand how to parent children. I try to distract her with plans for school.

While she's been in the hospital, we've connected to Fraser Academy, Vancouver's longest established private school for students with learning disabilities. It's mostly a school for kids coping with dyslexia while they struggle to learn to read.

I don't mention that Molly began reading adult books in grade 4; this isn't included on the educational assessments she's recently had which discovered an auditory language processing disorder. It's this disorder that qualifies her for admission. The school is very welcoming when we tour the classrooms and meet teachers. I explain that Molly is away but will visit the school later in the summer. Conveniently, it's late June, and secondary classes are over. Maybe they'll assume she's on a trip; I choose not to mention that the trip she's taking is to the local psychiatric unit.

As discharge looms with Molly still unstable, I begin to ask the nurses about resources in the community that might exist for us. The question seems to surprise each of them. I'm determined to adjust quickly to what's in store for Molly with this still mysterious illness.

Are there any support groups for parents? No one has heard of any. It takes over a year to learn about the family education course available to families through UBCs Schizophrenia Rehabilitation Day Treatment Program. It'll be two years before I find out that various branches of the BC Schizophrenia Society offer NAMIs Family to Family Education course. Each course is designed to include parents of children with bipolar disorder as well as schizophrenia.

When I walk by the CAPE unit, with its weekly arrival of newly psychotic children, I glimpse the strained faces of other parents. The C1 Assessment unit also has distressed parents visiting but there's no easy way I can connect to them. I wonder how other families, who've already been through this, have adjusted to the chaos of these unforeseen situations. Where are these families? Where are their stories which could help me get my bearings? Why can't I find them?

Just before Molly is released from Children's Hospital, we have a discharge meeting with the staff. We're surprised to see Veronica there until we understand that Molly has asked for her. When we enter the room, we see that she's already sitting close to Molly, showering her with warmth and solace.

I wonder if we should have been asked about the appropriateness of including her since we'll be billed by her for this involvement. I am tempted to mention the attitude towards psychiatrists that Veronica revealed to us, but, by now, I'm not sure who will be believed.

Dr. B tells us that we can get Molly's hospital records if we wish and before I can respond, Veronica is speaking. From her huddled position with Molly, she asks Molly if she'd like to see the records first so that she and Veronica can go over them together to see if there are things Molly would like to keep private.

This sounds great to Molly and this immediately becomes the new plan. Their request for the records never materializes, and it's several years before I realize I can ask Molly if she's willing to sign a paper requesting these so that we can look at them. There are no secrets in them, just the report of the phone call with Veronica labelling us as a dysfunctional family. She doesn't appear to have supplied any evidence, but this wasn't necessary for her words to look official on the report.

When Molly is discharged from Children's Hospital, Dr. B arranges for a follow-up appointment. We're grateful for how soon she will see Molly. Even though Molly is less agitated she is still furious with us. That fury is now focused on our decision to have her hospitalized.

We sit in Dr. B's waiting room while she meets with Molly. It looks as though it might be a struggle to get Molly to accept that she has a disorder and will need to be seen by Dr. B on a regular basis, but Dr. B soon calls us in.

We need to fire her, she says, since she's not able to do a good job with Molly. We learn that during the six-week hospitalization neither she nor any of the psychiatric residents have been able to establish any rapport with Molly.

This is so out of character for Molly; even though she's often found relationships with peers to be difficult to build, she's always responded enthusiastically to the high quality attention older kids and adults have been ready to give her. Dr. B tells us that when she and the residents tried to talk with Molly, she'd consistently put her hands over her ears, saying that psychiatrists play mind games and she won't listen to them.

Mind games? The unusual and undermining term that Veronica had used right in front of us to explain psychiatry to Molly. We try to explain to Dr. B; we just have to work harder for Molly to understand that Veronica couldn't really have meant that Molly shouldn't cooperate with the psychiatrists. We're having trouble since both she and we know that's exactly what Veronica meant and loyal Molly honours her mentors.

Fault Lines

Fall 2000-Winter 2000

I t's almost impossible to get an appointment with a child psychiatrist in Vancouver and Dr. B has managed to get us in to see Dr. Z. This appointment won't happen until early September and the prescriptions for Valproate can just be refilled until then. Molly has never had any of the difficulties some kids have with medications; she's never been allergic to anything and whenever she needed an antibiotic, whichever one was tried always worked. We understand that it can take many weeks for the medication to have its full impact, but we trust medications, and we're eager for Molly to be well again.

Molly does respond to the Valproate, even though she won't discuss what her diagnosis might mean. She's less agitated but is locked into her rage with us. If we loved her, we'd let her see Veronica. We obviously don't understand how much she really needs Veronica because we don't care about her feelings. I do know that Veronica accepts the existence of bipolar disorder; she's repeatedly told us how she worked to help her niece come to terms with her disorder. And surely Veronica would help in persuading Molly to attend Fraser Academy, a place Molly isn't sure she wants to go. Veronica must realize by now how inaccurate her instincts were about the nature of Molly's difficulties and she'll honour her professional responsibilities in dealing with a client with a serious mental illness. We will just keep a tighter rein on the situation and make it clear that the work we want her to do needs to focus on getting Molly to attend the one school that will be able to adapt to her. And given Veronica's ingratiating behaviour with the medical staff at the discharge meeting, she might be relieved in having a well defined task of helping Molly understand and accept her bipolar disorder.

We reduce her sessions from the once-a-week visits she's had over the past three years to every other week. Veronica is remote when we try to talk with her on the phone and we feel stuck but know that if we can just make it until September, Molly and we will be free of her.

Dr. Z is a fun, energetic guy who works hard to establish rapport with Molly when we finally get to meet with him. She looks ready to respond but a sour look closes up her face as she perhaps remembers her distrust of psychiatrists.

In the follow-up phone call, Dr. Z lets us know that he's talked to the therapist, thinks she's a jerk, and that we should end things with her right away. We find his bluntness refreshing but, in order not to further alienate Molly, we want to phase in with Dr. Z as we phase out with Veronica. Dr. Z refuses to start therapy with Molly as long as she's seeing Veronica; he'll see her weekly to manage her meds.

We make a bad decision. Molly says she doesn't like Dr. Z but agrees to go to him for the meds if she can keep seeing Veronica. We feel trapped. We can't seem to find out what has actually been happening with Veronica. Perhaps

Veronica has helped to develop Molly's acceptance of medication and maybe she even helped in persuading her to try out Fraser Academy. We can't be sure. Maybe we can gradually reduce her appointments with Veronica. Since Molly is seeing Dr. Z on a weekly basis for the meds, she might be able to bond with him.

We now know, from Molly, that none of these conversations with Veronica were about understanding bipolar disorder and its potential impact on her life. The focus was on helping her heal, with an eye movement technique, from the trauma of being hospitalized by us against her will; there wasn't any discussion of accepting the need for the hospitalization.

This kind of conversation could have helped alleviate Molly's rage towards us, a rage which was very dangerous for her to have at this point. Didn't Veronica understand that she was further undermining Molly's relationship with us when, finally, the source of her many difficulties was emerging?

Fraser Academy seems to be a good choice. Their lack of many group sports doesn't matter. Molly's earlier love of being on baseball, ringette and soccer teams has faded away; we'd wondered about the odd slowing of her movements that has occurred during the last couple of years. We're relieved that the classes seem as though they might be manageable. Also, she gets to meet daily with a counsellor who provides support for her growing difficulties with organizational tasks. The school's readiness to help with the difficulties of its students and its constant communication with us is unlike anything that would be able to happen in the overcrowded public schools.

I finally decide to tell the staff that Molly has a bipolar disorder. Their immediate and sympathetic acceptance astonishes me. They reassure me that their bipolar students often have trouble readjusting to school in the fall. Their bipolar students! I'm inspired by the possibility of making Molly's difficulties just be part of the spectrum of problems that a special school can tackle. I urge the staff to let the other parents of bipolar students know how much I'd appreciate making contact.

Their requests don't lead to the connections I yearn for with other parents; in a school devoted to accommodating kids with quirky brains, parents still want to keep this brain disorder secret. I will remember their reticence, their need to remain hidden, in future years when Sen. Michael Kirby discusses his decision to title his examination of Canada's broken mental health system *Out of the Shadows At Last*.

Molly does seem to like Dr. Z; it's hard to resist the boyish good humour which allows so many kids to work well with him. I've begun to hear from other parents about how well he communicates with their kids; the kids have ADHD and anxiety disorders, but Dr. Z has told us his practice also includes lots of adolescents with bipolar disorder.

I seek out Dr. Z's advice about planning a Christmas vacation. Two years earlier our family had a trip to a Caribbean resort which Molly relished. I wonder if this kind of sun drenched, relaxing environment could help our family regain the easy intimacy that's disappeared when any of us try to talk with Molly.

He's supportive. We call Molly into the room to let her know the good news. I remember to mention that both Mondimore's and Papolos' books on bipolar disorder are adamant that bipolar people should not drink any alcohol. We've learned from Naomi that, several times before Molly's psychotic break, she'd begun to explore whatever was in our infrequently used liquor cabinet and drink when we were away.

I've used Molly's fear of the hospital to discourage any use of alcohol and, at least with this issue, her older instincts to trust our suggestions have held sway. Remembering the resort's description of the on-site nightclub and its free alcohol, I ask Dr. Z to remind Molly that it's dangerous for people with bipolar disorder to drink.

Looking at the shy and troubled teen in front of him, he tells us to let her drink. These kinds of night clubs are safe; her sister will be with her, and she needs to let loose and have some fun. Molly glances at him with new enthusiasm. I decide to trust his judgement. He has lots of experience with bipolar teens. I wonder if authors of books might overreact to possible dangers in order to avoid lawsuits.

The silky white sand and intensely blue sky of Playa del Carmen promise to rescue us from the darkness of the previous spring, summer and fall. The girls have their own room nearby and the well-equipped resort with its expansive, lush grounds means they can easily stay within its safe confines. We're in time for dinner and we delight in exploring the abundant options. By the time we settle into our table, we're almost giddy as we give ourselves up to the colourful beauty that surrounds us. It looks like we are finally finding our way back to the happy shared excitement of our earlier trips together.

The girls don't protest as we all head to the resort's nightclub together. None of us minds the stale theatrics paraded on stage; just being in this fragrant, relaxed environment is all we need. The girls have a cocktail in front of them and we remind them that there should only be one more as Peter and I head to bed.

Naomi finds us early the next morning to explain what a hard time she had when we left. Molly's two cocktails made her feisty and she wandered away from her sister chaperon to sit at the bar and enjoy the attentive bartenders as she began ordering more drinks. It was several hours before Naomi could persuade a definitely drunk Molly to return to the room.

Molly sleeps late and we wait until after she's had breakfast to ask her about the previous evening. She glares at Naomi and tells us everything was fine and she won't need Naomi when she goes back to the club this evening. I remind her of the dangers of alcohol in the books I've read about bipolar disorder but a sullen wall has arisen and she's not listening.

We eat a late dinner and see if we can interest Molly in a walk along the beach afterwards. She lets us know that Dr. Z has approved of her 'clubbing' and we shouldn't interfere. Even though the club is nearby, we ask Naomi to lend her watchful eye and provide friendly companionship.

Naomi wakes us during the night; it's been even harder to get Molly back to the room. She's gotten even more drunk and argued loudly with Naomi who somehow managed to finally persuade her to return to their room. Peter and I talk through the night, outlining some kind of basic rules which we'll try to impose the next day. We'll distract her with a trip to Mayan ruins and search out family activities for the evenings. We want her to know that these kinds of evenings weren't what Dr. Z was envisioning; her behaviour could really become very dangerous for her.

We don't realize how dangerous it has already become until we see how strange Molly is the next day. We read on chairs near her room and almost don't recognize her as she slowly emerges from the doorway. Her long hair, wildly dishevelled from sleep, hasn't been brushed and her sweater makes no sense with her shorts; her shoe laces aren't tied. Even more frightening is her expression; she looks terrified, angry, and very suspicious.

We coax her into joining us for lunch. She keeps looking around the restaurant and is talking about the Mexican police. We wonder if they'd come on to the hotel grounds last night for some problem but gradually realize she thinks they are stalking her. When the food comes, she spits her first bite out of her mouth. She's onto us, she says. We're trying to poison her, she yells, as she bolts from the table.

As we watch her stumble through the lawns, we know her world and ours has shifted. Her manic break the previous spring revealed all the pressured speech, irrational anger, and flights of thought that we've come to understand as the psychosis a bipolar disorder can bring.

But this earlier break with reality doesn't resemble what we are now seeing. This is a depth of insanity we've never considered. It's as if she's earlier stepped slightly over some line that transgressed normality. Now, she's plunged into a roiling, utterly irrational, and disconnected state. Dr. Z has given me one tablet of Risperidone, an anti-psychotic, in case something went wrong.

We wait until she wanders back to her room in the early evening. We all join her, trying to soothe her with our voices. She's become even more obsessed about the Mexican police and seems open to our reassurances that we'll keep her safe from them. I show her the tablet that Dr. Z has given us in case she began to feel bad. Wouldn't she like to try it?

She considers it but then the suspicious look returns. She hisses that she'll never take anything from me; I'm just an irresponsible alcoholic.

The urge to laugh at this particular absurdity doesn't make it out of my mouth. Instead, we all try to get her to remember that I'm someone who doesn't actually like to drink alcohol and rarely even sips wine. When has she ever seen me drink a lot of alcohol?

She looks stronger as she begins to reveal her understanding of our family; she tells us that I am a secret drinker. I come home from work drunk and fall asleep. I shudder as I remember my restorative naps on Veronica's couch. Later, Peter and I talk about the bizarre story

Veronica wasted our time with in our family session with her. Apparently the account of her uncovering the source of a family's troubles when she discovered the mother's alcoholism wasn't just some way she wanted to impress us.

I return to our room to begin an unsuccessful search to find an earlier flight out of Cancun at Christmas. How are we going to get through the next four days and then onto a flight that can take us all back to the safety of Vancouver? What do people do in situations like this?

Molly's fear of the police keeps her close to her room and within our sight. I'm also relieved to have her out of sight from people who might think we should take her to a local hospital. We watch as Molly descends into a disturbing and disabling paranoia.

I can't get my bearings. I think about the three years Molly has spent with Veronica that have somehow culminated in Molly's accusation of me being an alcoholic. I am so lost that I begin to wonder if Veronica has indeed found something that could have contributed to this tragedy. My years of training in psychodynamic thought kick in. Could my lack of interest in drinking be because deep down I might have the potential to become an alcoholic. Maybe it was this potential that impacted Molly?

The reasoning, problem solving part of my mind rears up at this twisted logic. What if Veronica really just was abysmally ignorant about what she was seeing and rather than acknowledge this reality, she indulged herself with fantasies about her insights? I'm finished trying to appease Molly's unhealthy ties to this incompetent woman. We will put a firm end to this disturbing relationship but first we have to try to get our broken-looking daughter on the flight out of Cancun.

Naomi and I focus on helping Molly put on a sane looking combination of clothes. Even though she could pass for normal with a cursory glance, she's easily agitated and will never make it through the line-ups at the airport. What if I let the Air Canada staff know that my daughter is really unwell and ask for their assistance?

At the airport, I bring my request to the woman with the gentlest face. She doesn't even ask the dreaded question about what's wrong with my daughter; she pauses in her hectic routine, does a quick glance, and lets us know we'll be moved to the front of the line and boarded early. I love my adopted country more than ever.

We can manage this; we just have to get to the medical care we'll find back in Canada. Molly still has some understanding of what to do on the airplane and doesn't resist settling into her seat and putting on her seatbelt.

No one notices her until after the plane takes off and by then it must not be easy to turn the flight around. The stewardesses attempt to help us during the next five hours as we try to contain her urges to race down the aisles and kick the seat in front of her. Molly settles into focusing her growing rage onto Peter and me and won't talk to us; Naomi is left to try to keep her connected to any piece of reality she still can inhabit.

For the next three years, Naomi will be haunted by this trip. A previously enthusiastic traveller, she finds herself clenched with anxiety each time she flies. When she and we can finally get Molly off the plane, we all are hoping we'll never have to see anyone from that flight again.

Breakdown

January 2001 - February 2003

The hope for a quick solution in Vancouver doesn't materialize. Dr. Z is away on holiday and we finally enlist the help of a friend who's a psychiatrist; he is skilful in his ability to persuade Molly to begin taking an anti-psychotic. Although Molly's condition is terrifying, I know that bipolar disorder is treatable; we just need some kind of medication change.

Dr. Z looks shocked by the sight of Molly. We are so desperate for his help that I don't want to remind him of his error in judgement; I believe that in the future though, he might take the experts' predictions about the dangers of alcohol for bipolar patients more seriously. He apologizes for giving us such an ineffectively small dose of an anti-psychotic as we left the country. We let him know that, despite Molly's objections, we are now ending her relationship with Veronica and hope he will assume responsibility for her therapy as well as her medications.

Dr. Z is forthright about the limits of current psychiatric knowledge. Like many others, he sees it as a field that's just beginning to do the kind of research that's needed to help people with serious mental disorders. He introduces us to *The Broken Brain* by Dr. Nancy Andreasen, a biological psychiatrist, whose science based work in the 1980s was part of a movement that helped lead psychiatry out of its enmeshment with the Freudian theories which were not based on scientific research but that dominated psychiatry for most of the 20th century.

The unscientific approach to understanding serious mental illness not only deprived patients of truly helpful treatments but devastated families with unjustified blame. Families were not only blamed for causing these neurobiological disorders but, as they tried to help their ill family member recover, they found their efforts constantly undermined by suspicious mental health professionals who often pathologized their every interaction.

Psychiatry's wrong turn away from its science-based origins meant that the necessary brain research went unfunded for years. The result is that, although research demonstrates the genetic links and brain imaging techniques document the faulty brain functioning occurring in these disorders, the cures remain elusive. Dr. Z's open acknowledgement about the deficits in psychiatry is reassuring but also scary; will this mean that psychiatry's mastery of neurochemistry is too undeveloped to be able to fix what's wrong with Molly?

We know of Dr. Z's reputation for easily creating strong working relationships with his patients and we've seen him, all during the fall, cleverly try to build bridges to Molly. He tells Molly he wants to hear all about how annoying her parents are and he sends us out of his office to sit in the waiting room. Molly's hostility towards Peter, Naomi and me is relentless; we've felt helpless as we watch from such a far distance as she has become even more ill in the week we've been back.

Molly looks confused as she leaves Dr. Z's office. He calls us later to describe how hard it was to talk with her. He describes it like working with someone who's been brainwashed. Although Molly sees us as the source of her illness, he can't find any actual grievance about anything. She has no stories of mistreatment to share, just a kind of robotic insistence that we are a 'dysfunctional family full of secrets and lies,' the refrain that's returned to her since this new psychotic break in Mexico.

Fortunately, within a few sessions, Molly drops her rage towards us. On some level, she realizes something terrible is happening to her mind and she wants our help. This strong bond will see us through the horrors that the next two years will bring.

As the bond re-emerges, I remember an earlier incident when Molly's powerful, instinctive trust in us saved her life. When Molly was seven, we went sailing off Gabriola Island with friends. When we were back on the dock, Peter and Naomi were walking ahead of us as they carted supplies back to the car. I felt Molly clasp my hand and wondered, yet again, about the strong wish she had to stay in very close contact. Suddenly, she tugged at my hand and disappeared, with a startled cry, from beside me. The spaces cut out of the dock around the pylons were unnecessarily large; while looking at the boats, she'd walked right into the gap and was sinking below the water. I tightened my grip as my wrist was jolted and threw myself onto my stomach to reach my other hand around her small forearm that was just above the dock.

I shouted to Peter who by now must have already reached the parking lot and I kept shouting until two men from nearby boats looked up and came running. I couldn't pull Molly out of the water. I instantly knew that if we broke contact, she would drown. The hole she'd fallen through was too small for an adult to get through. The sides of the dock that extended down into the bay were long, the water was inky black, and no-one would be able to see her if she drifted down. What propelled her hand to clutch mine so tightly as the ground disappeared beneath her?

The men scrambled onto their stomachs, too, and together we pulled her out. Sputtering water, she was stunned from a bump to her head. She was too shocked to cry as we carried her to the car and back to our cabin where we finally stopped her shivering with dry clothes, lots of blankets and hot chocolate.

We aren't a family that throws itself into dangerous physical adventures and so we spent the evening trying to make sense of what had just happened in the ways that are familiar to us. We called the Silva Bay Marina to warn them of the danger; they were wary in their response, perhaps frightened of a lawsuit which we weren't planning. We spent the evening working on a letter to the Island newspaper, alerting others to the danger; we felt relieved to read it in the paper the following week.

It's a couple of weeks before Molly seems ready to try to return to Fraser. She is still frightened about the Mexican police but now talks more about the RCMP. Dr. Z has added to her dose of an anti-psychotic and believes that we're seeing the psychosis that comes when bipolar disorder isn't properly treated. He waits a few weeks before weaning her off the ineffective Valproate as he begins to introduce Lithium, the primary medication for treating bipolar disorder.

As I understand the long history of the drug, I wonder what might have happened if my father, a physician, had helped get my mother onto the drug forty years earlier. Or, if the psychiatrist she did briefly see had thought to try her on it instead of the several sessions of vague communication that resulted from his psychoanalytic approach.

Valproate had made Molly's hair begin to fall out and Lithium covers her face in acne. Both have weighed down her previously lithe body with an enervating fleshiness. With each increase in dose we think we are seeing improvement, but after several months it's obvious that Molly's illness is worsening. She cycles back and forth from a deathlike depression to the frantic pacing of mania.

Staff at Fraser Academy try to adjust to her declining ability to do any school work but by the spring of 2001, she's rarely able to attend any of her modified grade 10 classes and drops out. Dr. Z assures us that once we find the right way to treat her bipolar disorder, her symptoms will clear up. He begins to experiment with other of the anticonvulsants that in recent years have increasingly been used as mood stabilizers.

Nothing works.

Hamber House

Dr. Z then suggests that Molly spend a few weeks attending the summer day program at Hamber House. I've heard of Hamber House, but even as a long time Vancouver School Board (VSB) teacher I know little about this program that it helps fund. It operates as a collaborative effort with Children's Hospital and the Ministry of Children and Family Services for the twelve Vancouver adolescents with the most serious mental illnesses. I initially hate for her to identify with the teens she'll see there; she doesn't really belong since she's just waiting to spring back as we search for the right mood stabilizer. Some of these kids, burdened with rare disorders they've had since birth, have never had a normal life.

I acknowledge my ignorance when I tour the program and see the quietly troubled teens; Molly will be one of the most ill people there. Molly, restored to her lifelong habits of trusting the adults around her, is willing to attend.

Molly needs to be with people besides us and besides her classmates who also have mostly lost whatever abilities they had to socialize. She could benefit from young adults, youthful enough to resemble the friends she might have had if her illness hadn't claimed her, but they need to be people who understand her disorders. I remember the story of Clara Claiborne Park, a friend of my mother-in-law, who became a pioneer in rethinking autism.

I first met Clara Park at a family beach picnic on Block Island off the Atlantic seaboard. I watched her, curious, from a distance as I played with baby Naomi in the sand. So this was the woman who took on Bruno Bettelheim and his refrigerator mother theory of autism that dominated psychiatry for a good part of the second half of the 20th century.

We had read Bettelheim's explanation of how mothers cause autism at UCLA but not Clara's account in *The Siege* of trying to get help for her autistic daughter, Jessie. I was still attached that summer to my UCLA training in dance therapy even though I had doubts about the theories we had been taught.

Clara and one of her other daughters kept finding ways to warmly interact with Jessie, whose cold, mechanical demeanour frightened me. I needed to believe that all my intense reading on child development, my profound commitment, and my bountiful love would keep my child safe from this kind of grim condition.

As I watch Molly, my own equally troubling daughter twenty years later, I dig out Clara's book to see what it might offer. Clara's account of hiring students from Williams College, where she and her husband taught, to help with Jessie, grabs my attention. I begin to understand that, just like Clara, I could be Molly's case manager myself and try to organize some kind of rehabilitation program that at least could offer her some much needed companionship.

I put up ads at UBC's School of Rehabilitation Medicine for students interested in working with someone whose mental illness is severe. Over the next seven years, we will employ an incredible group of young women; most of them passed on the job to their friends as they graduated

57

from the programs or found full-time employment in their fields.

They are highly energetic, physically active women who seemed to take Molly's plight very much to heart. They were very inventive in helping Molly do whatever she was capable of at that point. Near the end of the two-year psychotic episode, that often meant just sitting near her in her almost catatonic state, radiating a loving presence, and a constant invitation to try to rejoin this world.

Because I was their employer, they communicated openly with me about whatever happened; there was no need for any inappropriate secrecy that can stymie parents in some treatment programs when the parents try to gauge progress or decline. Through the years, other parents become excited about this approach to a problem that they are also confronting.

By the fall of 2001, Molly's ability to understand or respond to the world around her has drastically declined. Dr. Z arranges for her to enter the day program at Hamber House on a full-time basis. An EEG that he has ordered at Children's Hospital reveals that Molly's brain's electrical patterns are aberrant.

The search for medications that might free her from her torment continues. There are parts of Hamber House that she's able to participate in. Her years of tennis lessons lead her to be drawn to the ping pong table and the staff often use this to try to energize her and help her focus. Her ability to do any school work is minimal. Even though she's often in a very volatile state, they welcome her.

Deanna Bader, the counselling psychologist at Hamber House, has trained with people outside of the Faculty of Education where she earned her MA. She knows a great deal about serious mental illness and will spend the next three years working hard to stay connected to Molly in the frenetic ride her illness will take her on.

Sometimes Molly cannot lift her head off her desk and, at other times, she is too agitated to even stay in the classroom. Whatever her illness is inflicting on Molly, Deanna is steadfast in her kindness, patience, and readiness to have Molly attend the program. Because I am still teaching every other day, we very much need access to a reliable environment where, at the very least, Molly can be safe. What do parents do who don't have access to this kind of haven?

It will take until the winter to finally stabilize Molly's mood by switching to Tegretol, one of the anticonvulsants that has become popular for treating bipolar disorder. As the months go on, it is becoming clear that even though Molly isn't being propelled through her extreme emotional roller coaster, she is becoming increasingly ill. Her thoughts are more disorganized and her delusions more severe.

Besides being paranoid about the police, Molly has begun believing that people can read her mind; this belief is excruciating to her. As well, she thinks that the radio is sending her messages; the messages are so disturbing that she needs all radios around her to be turned off. The practical implication of this experience with radios becomes complicated.

Molly is still able to respond to some physical activities and the staff work weekly with the students at a gym they rent at the nearby community centre. It takes a long time to persuade the community centre staff to occasionally turn off the radio so that Molly can bear to be in the workout room. I fluctuate between wanting the staff to try harder to get this accommodation from the community centre and being worried that they'll find Molly too difficult to have as a student.

Molly's mood disorder is responding to Tegretol but her worsening condition is terrifying to us. We expected her psychotic symptoms to fade away at this point but, instead, they are becoming worse. I know very little about schizophrenia, but I raise it as a possibility to Dr. Z by the spring of 2002. He first rushes to reassure me that it can't be schizophrenia; the long term prognosis would be too awful.

He then catches himself, acknowledges that he knows very little about schizophrenia and agrees that it is time to bring in more experts. He helps connect us to Jane Garland, the psychiatrist who heads the mood and anxiety disorders clinic at Children's Hospital; she is famous in the community for her expertise not only with treating serious mental illnesses but with her ability to work collaboratively with parents. We've become aware that the respectful, inclusive relationship we've had with Dr. Z is not common.

Jane is thorough in looking over all information about Molly and in her interviews with us. She suggests that Molly might have a schizoaffective disorder, a combination of both bipolar disorder and schizophrenia. In the midst of a situation that looks increasingly hopeless,

Jane tells us that the ongoing development of the brain through the early twenties could mean that Molly might get better. She suggests that Molly be seen by the group of doctors at the Refractory Psychosis Unit at St. Paul's Hospital.

Molly's case is presented to the group by Dr. Bill MacEwan, a national expert on schizophrenia. The team confirms the diagnosis of schizoaffective disorder and suggests raising the dose of her antipsychotic, Olanzapine. We wonder about asking Bill if he'll accept Molly as his patient but because he works at several hospitals, teaches at UBC, is involved in research and has been setting up the Early Psychosis Intervention program for Fraser Health Authority, he is rarely available.

He would only be able to see Molly once a month and we are desperate to continue with the weekly monitoring that Dr. Z provides. When we finally do begin working with Bill the following year, as Molly recovers from her psychosis, he tells me something shocking. During the assessment at St. Paul's, some of the team predicted Molly might have to be institutionalized for life. She was one of the most severely ill youth they'd seen in Vancouver.

The possibility of committing Molly to an institution is raised by both Dr. Z and by Hamber House's psychiatrist. I become frightened that Hamber House won't take her back for the following year and have no idea how we will manage. Molly vividly remembers her hatred of Children's Hospital and I have not forgotten the real dangers that can happen during hospitalized care.

Molly's comfort in our home is obvious and, even though she is becoming less and less capable of doing any of the simple tasks of daily living, we think it is healthier for her to remain with us. It will be years before I will fully realize the accidental wisdom of this decision to keep her with us in the home she's always known and loved. However, keeping Molly at home has become harder.

After she begins accidentally putting cups in the microwave for thirty minutes and keeps forgetting to turn off the faucets when she runs a bath, we can see that she cannot be left alone in the house. She also can no longer remember to watch out for cars if she tries to cross a street so she can't be outside by herself. We just have to cope until the summer when I'll be off work and we can figure out something else that we can try to treat Molly's catastrophic illness.

My ongoing support during these years is Deborah Simpson, an old friend who is an Occupational Therapist. I'd never understood exactly what an OT does besides helping people with physical disabilities find ways to adapt. I was very unfamiliar with OTs at this stage of Molly's illness, but now, after dealing with the mental health system for nine years, I have discovered OTs to be doing outstanding work in many psychiatric sites.

I think that their orientation to look for practical solutions to functional difficulties has led them to do some of the most innovative work in rehabilitation. They usually don't focus on interactions steeped in psychoanalytic and psychodynamic thought which, I believe, has been a great plus in liberating them to do some of the most truly useful work.

Deborah had been focusing for several years on working with people with the most serious mental illnesses. She's helped create Community Link, which employs consumers of mental health services as Peer Support Workers. They do outreach for more ill people who are isolated and need support to begin to interact with their community again.

I meet Deborah for coffee with the news from the St. Paul's Team. I decide to begin to investigate what a diagnosis that includes schizophrenia might mean. Although I've read every book I can find about bipolar disorder, after Dr. Z's comments, I haven't yet been able to start ordering material on schizophrenia. I can barely say the word without sobbing.

I bring to our discussion the weight of background knowledge about the disastrous history of treatment for the mentally ill. I'm very familiar with the mismanagement, both in the US and Canada, of the care for people with serious mental illnesses.

After the first generation of anti-psychotics began to be more widely used during the 1960s, the enormous and poorly functioning state mental institutions in the US began to close down; they were supposed to be replaced with community treatment centres that rarely emerged and tens of thousands of mentally ill people became homeless or committed crimes while ill; the prisons have become the new mental institutions in the US.

This same phenomenon occurred in Canada. The streets of Vancouver, especially the Downtown Eastside, are full of the neglected mentally ill. Street life has made it inevitable that they develop drug addictions and an entire new field is opening up to study and attempt to treat co-occurring disorders. I wonder if some part of this nightmare might become Molly's future.

Deborah tells me that her boss, Kim Calsaferri, has recently organized a workshop where staff learned about the Vermont Longitudinal Study. One group of researchers wondered about the unchallenged notion that schizophrenia is a progressively worsening disorder. Maybe institutionalization itself led to the decay of people's most fundamental life skills. The researchers decided to track down as many of the formerly institutionalized patients as they could locate in Vermont, believing that in this small state people might be easier to find.

The results astonished them and the psychiatric community. When the patients were received back into supportive environments, it looked as though people, in late middle age, began to get better. Deborah said more and more people in the US are beginning to talk about recovering from schizophrenia; it might even be possible for younger patients.

I've talked to a few of these Peer Support Workers and I sense that their illnesses haven't been as severe as Molly's. They had battled depression or had experienced a few psychotic symptoms. By now Molly has been deeply psychotic for over a year.

Hamber House has just had a speaker, a very articulate young man, who told the parent group about his journey to learn to deal with schizophrenia. I probe to hear exactly how psychotic he'd been and can't connect his struggles with what's happening to Molly. During the whole two years of Molly's increasingly debilitating psychosis, I will never find an example of someone recovering who has been as ill as she is.

Family Education

Deborah tells me that the University of British Columbia's Schizophrenia Rehabilitation Day Treatment Program provides an education course for parents even if our ill children aren't old enough to be in their program. I've avoided any conversations with her about the Day Program; I've seen how ill its patients are and, despite what's happening to Molly, I don't want this to be her next peer group. But news of an education program for families feels like a gift from the heavens.

When the first of the education classes start, Peter and I are relieved to be surrounded by people who know exactly what we are going through. Lectures by Dr. R provide the background that we need to have about the neurophysiology of schizophrenia. Learning about the basics of schizophrenia is reassuring; we get to see that people have been working hard to unravel this disorder that now dominates our lives.

The illness has positive symptoms which refer to disorders that are added on to the person who is suffering. These can include delusional thinking, ideas of reference,

65

disorganized thoughts and speech, and hallucinations. Molly's terror of police following her, the belief that people can read her mind, her jumbled thoughts and her disorganized behaviour all make sense now.

The negative symptoms of schizophrenia are what the illness takes away including affect, motivation, speech and thought. These are harder losses to assess because she's very withdrawn much of the time which, in itself, is a negative symptom. We don't learn at this point about the development of the predictable cognitive deficits which will trouble us in years to come.

Dr. R is understandably very concerned about preventing relapses in patients who have been stabilized. He explains how important families are in helping to keep their ill family member on medication. But then he goes on to explain the literature about Expressed Emotion, or EE, and schizophrenia. Research, he tells us, shows that families that have high levels of expressions of negative emotion and criticism have higher rates of relapse in their family member.

Since it was quickly apparent when she was becoming ill that Molly could not tolerate the slightest feedback that could be considered critical, it had been very clear to us that this should never happen. Before we'd understood that she was actually ill, I'd reminded her when she was emptying the dishwasher, that certain pieces of cutlery always went in a different drawer, and she'd become enraged. I hadn't known that soon she wouldn't even be sure what the dishwasher was. Perhaps this hadn't been as obvious for some families and so it might be valuable to provide the basic communication tips Dr. R focused on. ("Always use 'I' statements in communicating with your family member.") I remember thinking that it must have been hard in doing this research to distinguish between the high rates of stress families display when coping with a family member who is in the midst of a relapse on the one hand from habitually high stress levels within a family that could precipitate a relapse on the other.

It's only much later, when I finally discover Dr. Fuller Torrey's *Surviving Schizophrenia*, that I see the Canadian research that was especially significant in debunking the EE theories. Fuller Torrey sees a lot of this work as just one of many efforts to find new ways to blame families.

During the course, I feel my strength return to me as I handle the notebook full of materials we've been given. Missing from the course are the presentations from consumers who have recovered and families who have gone through this process with them. I am so disoriented at this point that it doesn't even occur to me until years later how essential these elements are to a program that is intended to offer families the best possible support and help them experience hope.

Nevertheless, we are back in a world that is familiar to us. Overwhelming problems can be studied, solutions can be attempted, and progress can be made. The word 'schizophrenia' isn't as frightening as it has been, but the future is still murky. By now Molly can no longer bathe herself; even though she can still put shampoo in her hair, she can't understand how to get it out except with a towel.

Riverview

One of the mothers in the group is especially articulate. Barbara Forster-Rickard, an instructor at Vancouver Community College, has a daughter who is in something called locked care. Brittany had been a bright, creative girl until at fifteen she became obsessed with killing herself. For two years, she's needed the safety of 24-hour care to keep her alive while the search for better medications to treat her schizoaffective disorder goes on. Brittany is finally being stabilized as a result of the work by the psychopharmacologists at Riverview Hospital and makes weekend visits home.

Talking with Barbara is exhilarating and we become friends. I examine her closely to see how she is coping with each aspect of her ordeal. Managing life threatening crises is just another skill she's acquired; I'm inspired by her courage. When Barbara asks if I can pick up Brittany at Riverview for a weekend afternoon while she visits her family in Germany, I'm pleased to get the chance to help. I'm also yearning to see just what it is that some psychiatrists have thought would be good for Molly.

Riverview first opened, using temporary buildings, in 1904, on 1,000 acres in rural Coquitlam. Its first permanent building, the Hospital for the Mind, opened with 300 patients on its site in 1913 and was considered state of the art in psychiatric hospitals at the time. Both a provincial experimental farm as well as a provincial botanical garden were included on the grounds. At its peak in 1951, it housed over 4,600 patients. By the 1990s, most of the patients had been moved out and many of the buildings had been closed. The building that Molly and I approach may have been beautiful once but its aging, neglected facade suggests decay more than the restoration of health.

Sitting on a front stoop is a group of middle-aged people who look ravaged. A couple of them twitch spasmodically with the symptoms of tardive dyskinesia which the older anti-psychotics often caused. One woman's tongue keeps drifting in and out of her mouth. These are sights I'd encountered in Los Angeles when I'd trained in psychiatric units and they illustrated what the worst of mental illness and its treatment could bring.

The overflowing ashtrays speak to the countless days spent on this stoop waiting for something to happen. It seems as though these unlucky people are just hoping nothing will happen since life in the outside world has been so impossible for them. Molly stays close to me as I ask for directions to Brittany's ward.

"Is she staying here?" an older woman asks, pointing at Molly with her cigarette. "You dropping her off?" Molly doesn't look as troubled by this assumption as I am. I've ensured that Molly is well dressed and well groomed. But there is no fooling these experts. They know a really sick person when they see one.

"We're just picking up a friend," I say, keeping my voice from breaking. "We're not staying."

"Never! Never! Never!" I shout inside myself. I will not give Molly up to this fate. I will quit my job. I will read more books, consult more experts, find more ways to stimulate her brain. We could investigate getting Molly onto clinical trials of new medications that look promising.

The word "recovery" is now in my frame of reference and I wonder what it could mean in the future. Her brain physically exists even if it has turned into a jumble of tangled neural pathways. Don't people recover from brain injuries and from strokes? I recall stories of people sitting for weeks and months by the bedside of someone in a coma; isn't there some evidence that sometimes some piece of the coma victim's brain registers their presence and this helps bring them back to consciousness?

I wish I had a guidebook for this overwhelming journey. There is one thing I am certain of: as long as Molly can possibly understand anything, I want her to experience every day that we are working to liberate her from the prison her mind has become.

When we get home, Brittany is easygoing, ready to eat lunch on the back deck. The summer sun warms us and, later, both girls look interested when Naomi arrives and suggests they make collages. She's spread a tantalizing array of magazines across the dining table inside and scissors, glue and construction paper are arranged for easy access.

Brittany quickly assembles an expressive collection of images and considers various arrangements on her paper. She is very purposeful as she works, and, if the sun didn't catch the gleaming white scars that line her arms, there would be little trace of mental illness.

Molly looks puzzled and, with lots of encouragement from Naomi, picks up the scissors, but as she tries to arrange her hand around the handle, it's as if they are something she's never seen before. I leave Molly at home when I take Brittany back to the hospital that evening. I don't want any part of her getting used to making this trip.

Molly's connections to the world around her are withering. She can still play ping pong which we've now set up in the basement but she can return fewer balls. And she's losing words so that the playful sounds of the name for the activity she can still enjoy have disappeared. She has begun making a tentative gesture with her hand and says "that game" when she wants to play. She speaks less and less and often doesn't seem to hear people who are trying to talk with her.

By now she's tried almost all of the medications; Dr. Z hoped the combination of Tegretol which keeps her mood stabilized and the 40 mg of the anti-psychotic Olanzapine would snap her out of her psychosis. The St. Paul team has approved this approach. However, some deep force of nature is dragging her away from the world around her; she is disappearing more and more from herself and her life.

My broken heart is becoming harder to control. I start weeping at inconvenient times and places. During dinners in restaurants with friends. During a play where the main character is dying. Walking by any park where jubilant young girls race around playing soccer as Molly used to love to do.

On the days I don't teach, I drop Molly off at Hamber House and return home. I try to see where I am, what I want to do in the midst of the growing suffering of our loss.

When I allow myself to picture how Molly was and how little is left of her, I wail. For hours. For days and weeks and months. I wonder if this well of anguish will ever run dry. I search the endorphined calm that finally comes at the end of each plunge into the core of my agonizing grief. I want to see if there are any thoughts that accompany this fleeting peace that I can hold on to.

I can't find any, but slowly it feels as though some of my basic cells are incorporating the brutal new truth. I try out sentences to say to myself. "Molly might be one of the many people who never recover from their psychosis. At least, she had a happy childhood. More research is being done all the time." I speak the words slowly, forcing my mouth to accept their sounds. But I can never get through them without the sound of gasping sobs breaking the air.

The Menninger Clinic

What if we took her to a clinic in the US? We've learned enough to know that new medications are released there sooner and that the larger population means psychiatrists have even more experience in working with refractory psychoses like Molly's.

Peter's cousin Stephanie, a psychiatrist at Harvard, recommends the Menninger Clinic in Topeka, Kansas. It's been around since the 1920s, but I've always associated it with the most orthodox of Freudian models. Even if it's evolved, I imagine it full of the psychodynamic thought that's already contaminated the early damaging interventions Molly's received; these are the Freudian-based theories that gave me a worse than useless background for understanding the catastrophic brain disorders which we're confronting. Stephanie assures us that Menninger has changed with the times and that its practices are based on the latest brain research.

Stephanie's knowledge helps me not worry about the preliminary paperwork Menninger sends. The extensive questions about toilet training are predictable and sad. The whole history of psychiatry, which I'm now beginning to view from a very different perspective, is tragic.

I haven't yet come across one of the key books that will give me much needed perspective; it's by a Canadian. University of Toronto Professor Edward Shorter has written *A History of Psychiatry* which documents how psychiatry in the 20th century strayed from medicine's scientific foundation and only in the latter part of the century began to try to make up for the years of neglected research opportunities.

This is our first plane trip with Molly since the manic havoc of our return flight from Cancun. This time Molly is very subdued. I'm not sure how much of the purpose of this trip she understands. I think she just instinctively trusts that we are trying to free her from the mental chaos that haunts her days.

The sight of the rolling hills and the stately brick buildings that fill the campus of the Menninger Clinic buoys us with hope. It's such a kind, gentle and orderly atmosphere, at least on the surface. Menninger has not told us that they are in the midst of closing down this site and are moving to Texas to become part of Baylor University's Department of Psychiatry.

Most of the impressive buildings are empty and some of the services we're expecting, like a long-awaited MRI, aren't available. Nevertheless, the basic mechanisms of the thorough assessments they've been specializing in are in place. For five days our mornings and afternoons are filled with meetings with an impressive team of experts who meticulously review every aspect of Molly's early and recent life. This high quality, sustained examination of Molly's illness and our experiences with her does not resemble anything we've experienced or heard of in Canada.

One of the first very informative sessions is our meeting with their educational consultant. Unlike the people who had done the educational assessments with Molly in Vancouver, she is an international expert on the cognitive dimensions of serious mental illnesses. Her comments finally make sense of a big piece of the puzzle.

Of course Molly didn't suddenly develop serious learning disabilities. The cognitive decline we had been witnessing for several years before her psychotic break was caused by the prodromal phase of schizophrenia. I've agonized over our decision to give Molly the anti-depressants that led to her psychotic break. By now the news is full of stories of the potential of SSRI's like Paxil to trigger mania in people with a history of bipolar disorder in their extended family. This psychologist and the psychiatrist believe that the Paxil did cause the manic break but that the chaos of the schizophrenic part of her illness was already brewing.

The social worker encourages us to connect to the National Alliance for the Mentally Ill (NAMI). I've vaguely heard of this group which is the largest advocacy group in the world for people with serious mental illnesses and their families. I'm not interested in advocating for anything; I just want some better medications.

I learn that NAMI was started 20 years earlier by a group of parents and mental health professionals who had ill family members and knew that the mental health system was completely inadequate. A central figure in NAMI is E. Fuller Torrey, a world-renowned research psychiatrist who had balked at the destructive impact of Freudian thought which had dominated psychiatry for most of the 20th century.

Neurobiological approaches to these illnesses had been ridiculed and received almost no funding during this time. With the help of NAMI and independent-minded psychiatrists like Torrey, more research about serious mental illnesses is happening. With this introduction, I can finally open a copy of Torrey's *Surviving Schizophrenia, A Manual for Families, Patients and Providers* and discover the intellectual and emotional home for which I'd been searching.

This book still remains the seminal work endorsed by the Schizophrenia Society of Canada. A researcher himself, Torrey is also a master of combining both cutting edge research and historical background into a coherent big picture. He's forceful in discussing the enormous damage that has been done to consumers and families because of the family-blaming theories.

Torrey's approach to schizophrenia is clear: "There is no evidence whatsoever that schizophrenia is caused by how people have been treated either as children or as adults; it is a biological disease of the brain, unrelated to interpersonal events of childhood or adulthood."

Torrey's summaries of the genetic contributions to the development of schizophrenia are comprehensive. It's widely understood now that genes don't completely control the development of the disorder. Other factors play an important role. This wiggle room makes some writers eager to again look to family experiences as the key environmental factor; old theories seem to have a hard time fading away.

However, as time goes on I will come across considerable research that suggests many other contributing factors. Eventually I will compile a long list which research is identifying as significant.

Peter was an older father; Molly was conceived in UCLA's family student housing which, located at the intersection of two freeways, had a high lead level. I had the flu during my pregnancy. Molly's delivery was botched. Her December birth fits in with the unusually high number of winter births of people who develop the disorder.

Despite its origins in Freudian explanations, there is not a hint of family blaming at Menninger's. They speak with Dr. Z and praise his supportive attitudes. However, our confidence quickly fades as they explain what they think about the treatment Molly has received. She's never been given a high dose of an anti-psychotic. They say they've seen this slow approach with Canadian psychiatrists before.

Apparently American psychiatrists try to get people quickly out of a psychotic state by using much higher doses of anti-psychotics much sooner. There's some evidence that psychotic states are toxic to the brain and the aberrant neural pathways occurring in psychotic states can become more ingrained the longer they last. This is gloomy news since Molly is well into the second year of this worsening psychosis.

We leave with a new plan. The dose of Olanzapine can still be raised and, if this doesn't work, they want Molly to be weaned off Tegretol which will be necessary for her to try the drug of last resort, Clozapine. This drug can cause a drastic reduction in white blood cells in about 1% of people. Called agranulocystosis, it means that people taking it require regular blood tests. But what will happen without the Tegretol, the solution that finally freed Molly from the emotional frenzy of her bipolar disorder? Olanzapine has just been approved by the US FDA as a mood stabilizer as well as an anti-psychotic.

What Menninger doesn't tell us is some of the most crucial information we need at this point. They feel Tegretol is unnecessary and convey some undefined dissatisfaction with it as a drug. We think it is because almost all of the anticonvulsants can be "cognitive dimmers" that limit the basic thinking processes that are already so damaged. They don't tell us that Tegretol has been reducing the absorption of the Olanzapine by up to 50%. I still don't know why the psychiatrists who worked with us never mention this since their major conclusion is that Molly has yet to experience the effect of a high dose of an anti-psychotic.

Maybe they assume that the primary psychiatrist is taking these drug interactions into account in his treatment strategy. Or, family friendly as they seem to be, they still don't understand that families want to be told all information that could possibly be relevant; this approach could truly empower families in making the decisions that will confront them. Providing all of the information that families need also means that families are in a better position to keep track of crucial information that an overworked mental health system doesn't record well.

Dr. Z is eager to support the new plan. We'll continue to raise the Olanzapine up to 60 mg through the fall and slowly reduce the Tegretol in case we have to introduce Clozapine.

The Playwriting Contest

Menninger's careful attention and sympathetic stance to what this illness has meant for all of us has empowered me. I decide to take another unpaid leave of absence from work and attempt something new. As a long-time secondary school drama teacher focusing on social realism, I know that I've never come across a script that deals accurately with schizophrenia.

A thorough search of the Playwrights Union of Canada catalogue confirms this troubling vacuum. Putting on plays with my east Vancouver students has always been an uplifting though hectic experience and being around a creative focus again could reintroduce the joyfulness that has disappeared from my life. I decide to make use of some funds I've inherited to sponsor a national playwriting contest.

Peter's family's history of epilepsy may have contributed to the genetic background for Molly's illness, but I know I am the major carrier of the genes that have wrought havoc on Molly's life. I love the idea of using something else I've inherited to improve the social context in which this cruel illness is being played out.

Playwrights' Theatre Centre (PTC) in Vancouver agrees to be a co-sponsor of a national playwriting contest and to put on a professionally staged reading of the winning scripts for two nights. The prize money for the winning playwright and the two runners-up might ensure active participation from professional playwrights who, in the process, will become much more knowledgeable about schizophrenia in all of their future work. The BC Schizophrenia Society (BCSS) and the Schizophrenia Society of Canada (SSC) become co-sponsors and advertise the contest on their websites.

I'm very explicit in the conference guidelines that playwrights need to educate themselves about the research that focuses on the neurobiological origins of schizophrenia. I'm not eager to promote yet another avenue for the too common literary trope of mentally ill young adults coming to terms with their childhood abuse. This was all I had ever been really educated in and so was completely unprepared for the reality that planted its bleak self in front of us.

I call the event the *This Is a Spoon One-Act Playwriting Contest*. Molly, the previous winter, had begun trying to save some sense of the world by naming things.

"That's a tree. Those are trees," she would repeat as she looked out the living room window. She used to love to make pasta but the complexity of the task was well beyond her, when, one evening, she picked up her favourite pasta serving spoon. She clutched it telling herself, "This is a spoon. A spoon! A SPOON!" It was as if her efforts could help her hold on a little longer to her grasp on a world that was being pulled away from her.

The development of the contest proceeds well until I get a call from the PTC to come into their office. They unfold a scathing letter in front of me that has scared them. One of the many members of PTC has written to protest the conference guidelines. He's adamant in maintaining that there's no evidence that schizophrenia is a neurobiological disorder. In fact, the whole notion of mental illness has been invented by psychiatry and pharmaceutical companies to make money.

All antipsychotics do is sedate people who are just expressing themselves and are labelled by a rigid society as being ill. I'm very familiar with this way of thinking but now realize how ignorant it is. This anti-science approach has again been flowering with careful cultivation from misguided sociologists who think they are freeing troubled people from the labels that they see as the source of their trouble. I'm eager to share all of the brain-based research I've been discovering with the letter writer, with the staff at

PTC, and with anyone else who will listen to me, but this isn't what's wanted.

PTC is reeling from the accusation of not welcoming all points of view and changes their website to accommodate their critic. Happily, the websites of the BCSS and the SSC are very pleased to keep the original version of the call for science-based scripts posted on their websites.

The contest continues to generate interest across the country with many scripts coming from people who live with these disorders. They don't seem to think their problems are all about being falsely labelled with an illness; they believe they have an illness and they'd like it to be better treated and better understood by the people around them.

I wish all of the anti-medication ranters could have seen firsthand what happened over the winter in our home.

Breakthrough

Winter 2003 - Spring 2003

I don't really pay attention to the first signs of change. Although the previous two years of Molly's psychosis had been a long slope down, it wasn't a smooth line. The small jagged peaks would often come with a switch in medications or for other still mysterious reasons. Molly would become a little livelier or a little more lucid but these slight fluctuations wouldn't last. I'd learned to cushion myself from the wrenching loss that would follow the rebirth of hope with these short-lived improvements.

In December 2002, Molly's teacher at Hamber House tells us how surprised he is that Molly has begun to participate in PE classes and knows how to play soccer. Since Molly played soccer for several years, it's not a surprise that somewhere in her she remembers what to do during one of her livelier periods.

Rosie, one of Molly's dedicated support workers, also tells me how excited she was when Molly didn't tell her to be quiet all during their long afternoon together. It had become the pattern that, although Molly would accompany Rosie for outings designed to invigorate her in any way possible, Molly would quickly tell her to stop her constant efforts to promote conversation.

Molly needed to pay attention to elaborately irrational thoughts that she would, much later, try to explain to us. Rosie feels there's some kind of breakthrough because Molly didn't tell her to stop talking and although she didn't say much, she seems to have heard more of what Rosie kept offering.

The breakthrough I witness occurs in February. Molly has slowly been weaned off Tegretol all fall and we are now seeing Bill MacEwan to initiate Clozapine. Dr. Z readily acknowledges his lack of expertise in dealing with a schizoaffective disorder and has never worked with Clozapine. Bill MacEwan is a widely respected expert on schizophrenia. Under his guidance, Molly has begun a miniscule dose of Clozapine and we've signed up for the elaborate blood tests to watch for signs of agranulocytosis.

One afternoon Molly is sitting in the chair in the living room where she spends vast amounts of time rarely moving or speaking. I know I should read more about catatonia but at this moment I am reading a soul-nurturing novel.

The steadiness in Molly's voice startles me. "My head feels so much clearer." So many words and they haven't been coaxed out of her. She is looking at me with a firm gaze. "My head is clearer."

I squash the hope impulse that has gotten out of hand so many times before.

"Oh. Does it feel good?"

She is still completely present. "Yes."

I can't remember the next piece of the conversation. I know it was about little things as I cautiously test how deep these changed waters are. She keeps responding in ways that make sense. I feel as though she has returned from hell. And as the miraculous afternoon goes on, she seems to be looking for some explanation for what has been happening.

I watch her as I show her the short BCSS "Reaching Out" video which tells the story of several people recovering from schizophrenia and has several local psychiatrists, including Bill MacEwan, explaining the disorder. She is taking everything in. She is mentally frail and a little frightened but is now sharing our world.

I don't call Peter but wait for him to come home from work and see what's happening. We both try to contain our excitement and just casually respond to our daughter who has risen from the dead.

After a few days, I decide to further test the depth of the change. One of Molly's horrific and persistent delusions is that people can read her mind. I've read in child development literature that this is an early belief as infants grow in their consciousness. The illness has trapped her in this agonizing belief for almost two years.

"Molly, you know that idea about people being able to read your mind. Do you think people can do that?"

She pauses. "People can't read my mind." Then she remembers. "Why did I think that?"

"It was your illness, but now you're better."

The *Globe and Mail* article I'd recently written about her is in the living room. I show her the interesting drawing of her the Globe's illustrator has done. I point to the paragraph about the *This Is a Spoon Playwriting Contest* that's happening, but she's not up to reading a line of words. She listens as I describe the contest, and the performance of a staged reading of the winning script that will be happening in several months.

"Can I come?"

"Of course," still not totally believing this is happening. Is life now going to allow her to stay well and give our family the gift of being together for this important event?

"Why is it called the Spoon?"

She doesn't remember anything about the weeks and weeks when she desperately tried to name the pieces of the confusing world that was slipping away from her. We are discovering that huge chunks of the last two years just aren't available in whatever memory bank she's using. I'm not sorry; why re-experience the terrors of this time when she's now so interested in the world she is seeing anew. Pieces of these experiences do gradually return later and she is better equipped to handle the disturbing memories.

We haven't told Bill MacEwan about the lifting of her psychosis when we arrive to increase the dose of Clozapine. As he experiences the transformation, we all keep smiling at each other. But, he's perplexed. The tiny dose of Clozapine can't really be doing this, can it? We've learned that brains are very unpredictable in their responses to medications and many psychiatrists have told us how difficult it is to know how to treat Molly's brain. We're all delighted to raise the dose and later taper off the Olanzapine.

The delights don't last.

The Clozapine fills Molly's mouth with pools of saliva that drip out and that make her feel like she's choking. She is still unable to handle difficulties and I try to persuade her that these side effects can fade. We don't want to let go of this breakthrough but Molly can't cope. After two weeks, she insists on seeing Bill to get off the Clozapine.

I want Bill to find a magical way to persuade her to stay on the Clozapine. Aren't psychiatrists supposed to be good at this? Molly is adamant; she won't take any more Clozapine. She's always choking and feels as though she can't breathe. Bill reluctantly agrees to discontinue the Clozapine. I prepare for the worst.

The worst must be waiting nearby but it's not stepping in the door. The 60 mg of Olanzapine is keeping her psychosis away. However, now her physician is worried about her suddenly high prolactin levels and I decide to revisit Eli Lilly's website on Olanzapine. I'd been vigilant during the first year in reading all of the information on the websites of the constantly changing array of medications Molly's tried.

The lists of possible side effects and complicated drug interactions are only cause for more worry. I'd stopped reading them and just waited to see if anything would actually work. Smaller problems could be dealt with later. Later has arrived and I need to see if the Olanzapine is causing the elevated prolactin levels. I discover that it is, but the Eli Lilly website offers much more. It solves the mystery. The attempt over the previous year to finally give Molly a high dose of an antipsychotic had been doomed. The Tegretol she was also taking has been interfering with its absorption by up to 50%.

Maybe Molly never actually had a refractory psychosis; until we'd taken away the Tegretol, she'd never received a really high dose of an anti-psychotic. This oversight will continue to haunt me. I'm not sure that even if I'd read this earlier, I would have known what to make of it; I never felt qualified to assess which pieces of information were actually significant.

I will keep wondering about what would have happened if she'd received this high dose early on. Not only would she have been spared the agonies of the two years of disintegration; maybe she wouldn't need the problematic high doses of anti-psychotic that become essential to keep psychosis away.

I wonder if the course of Molly's illness and of her life could have been much different if we'd never sent her to Veronica. Veronica's undermining of Molly's relationship with Dr. B early on in her illness meant that Molly didn't have access to a psychiatrist with expertise in treating schizophrenia.

We rejoice. We didn't know if her psychosis was treatable and now feel like she's been given a second chance at life. However, we are well aware that many people don't respond to any existing medication. I think of the families who are still waiting, looking to see what will happen with drugs that are in clinical trials when they finally become available.

Molly is fragile and easily confused if ideas or communications are complicated. But she really is back. Even her smile is returning; this smile had always been remarkable to people. So big and open. So honestly present in her expression of gladness. How can she be so wholeheartedly welcoming to life when it's spent years insisting she live in her own private hell?

She wants to learn things. She doesn't understand how little she understands. She is now 18 with an education that was floundering by the time she entered grade 8. She still can't seem to find many words. I get a book of elementary-aged crossword puzzles and each afternoon we work on them. She can't come up with the words herself but recognizes them as they appear, adding to her pile of reacquired knowledge. She can't read and doesn't seem to want to be read to but she begins to listen again to all of the conversations in the house and is tracking them. I had never realized what a sophisticated skill this is until it had disappeared.

She wants to hear again and again about her illness. We just say she has schizophrenia because it's still too hard for her to understand the complexities of a schizoaffective disorder. We wait for the predicted grief and anger but they're not appearing. She's just curious and incredibly relieved to be released from the terrifying delusions that had tormented her for so long.

She brings a childlike innocence to her acceptance that she has a lifelong disorder but she is trying to understand the words 'schizophrenia' and 'mental illness' and put them into the bigger picture of the world that she is reconstructing. She does tap into earlier associations with schizophrenia one afternoon. We are driving down Main Street to the grocery store when her attention is caught by a homeless man in the corner of the parking lot who's rearranging the clutter in his shopping cart.

"Will I be getting a shopping cart?"

I park the car and will my voice to be convincingly certain as I take on this assumption that is said with a heartbreaking naivete.

"No, these are sick people who don't have a family to help them."

I already know how simplistic this explanation is. Some parents I've met have children who don't understand that they're ill and refuse treatment. The only reason they don't have a family to help them is because of a broken system that honours their right to be sick. I don't even want Molly to know this is a possibility. We are going to walk into the grocery store to find delicious food to cook for dinner and away from this parking lot where mental illness thrives.

I know I need help in coming to terms with what is happening. I have tried various sources of support during the previous two years. I have been having almost weekly walks with my friend Rhoda and, although she's consistently generous, I know I must be a burden. I've always prided myself on being a great listener in my friendships but, since Molly's illness, I have a hard time attending to topics outside of our immediate crises.

Rhoda is a historian and I've been consistently intrigued by her energetic explanations of her research into the situations of medieval women. As Molly has become more ill, I realize I can't follow Rhoda's accounts; the horror of Molly's situation holds the centre of my attention and I'm no longer being an equal partner during our walks. I know this level of need is too much strain on a friendship that should have much greater reciprocity. I also see how much I am slipping away from parts of my own life.

Already familiar with the therapeutic process, I have received recommendations for two therapists. Both women are very nice but each is steeped in training that leads them to want to help me examine my already well-explored childhood experiences.

I need help managing the daily difficulties and adjusting to the constant uncertainty. From various comments these women make, I can see that they know even less about serious mental illnesses' impact on families than I do. It's only when I will later make contact with NAMI that I will see that a whole body of literature has been developing about the journey of the family in coping with serious mental illnesses and that these well meaning women hadn't had a clue about its existence.

I appreciate having a safe place to grieve that doesn't further burden my friends but each session costs the equivalent of six hours of high quality recreational therapy for Molly, which actually provides me much greater relief.

I've visited a family support group that one of the community mental health teams makes available to any family coping with a serious mental illness. I do learn a lot from this group especially because the leaders often bring in speakers.

Peter never wants to return after he goes with me to our first session which focuses on a staff member reading Shel Silverstein's story, *The Giving Tree*, to us. The moral of the story is that parents must stop giving in to an endlessly needy child who will only destroy them in the end. This choice of a story strikes us as odd since we're adjusting to Molly being profoundly psychotic and our need to completely rearrange our lives in order to find a way to rescue her from this catastrophe.

We know enough to not even utter the word 'rescue' since it is a dangerous code word signifying the kind of co-dependent relationships every therapist is trained to fix. In spite of our limited knowledge, we can see that just practising tough love is an utterly inappropriate response to our situation. I will always be grateful that, despite our confusion, we knew enough to realize that this advice would not help us or Molly.

One of the group leaders, Ann Webborn, invites a therapist from Family Services of Greater Vancouver. I've always wondered what exactly they do and whom they serve. I'd been growing impatient about an array of poorly informed mental health professionals I'd encountered who were overly confident in thinking they had something to offer, and I hope we'll learn about a valuable new resource.

After the woman describes all the help this fee-for-service organization offers individuals, couples and families in trouble, I ask her what training she and the staff have about serious mental illnesses. I explain that most people who are attending this group are trying to live with psychotic children and ask about her expertise in this area.

Other parents began to question her assumption that traditional family therapy techniques, like identifying over involvement with children, can be helpful to us in our situations. After she acknowledges that she and her staff don't actually have any training in serious mental illnesses,

I ask if the staff will be receiving professional development on this topic. I don't say, but probably should have, that there's a good chance that some families that approach them might actually be dealing with serious mental illnesses and their ignorance is probably causing dangerous delays in getting appropriate treatment. She has, not surprisingly, become defensive and says they are too busy for this kind of training.

When she leaves for the second part of the evening, Ann apologizes. Ann, a very experienced OT who actually knows a lot about mental illnesses and the kinds of difficulties we're facing, hadn't realized this woman thought this basic knowledge wasn't necessary. I'm proud of the group that has dared to ask for expertise in people who should have it.

Finally, I decide to invite ten mothers of children with serious mental illnesses to my home. I've met these women during the previous two years at the UBC and BCSS courses, at conferences, and through the grapevine. I tell them that I'd like them to spend an evening hearing five - minute synopses of each other's stories about their ill children.

From the courses I've taken on group process, I know that it will be important to have some core structures and boundaries in place. Each woman must be guaranteed time to speak. All of the women I invite have already acquired fundamental knowledge about the brain disorders affecting their children.

As I had hoped, by the time we've gone around the circle, the women are exuberant. All of us are feeling the healing power of being in a group of supportive people who deeply understand what we are going through. When I ask if anyone would like to be part of a monthly support group, everybody is interested. After four years, I will start another group with ten other women because the first group has invested so much in learning each other's complicated stories, that they haven't wanted to expand.

Through these groups I begin to put my experiences into new perspectives. It's frustrating to see how many of these committed and resilient mothers have had to deal with and continue to encounter the ongoing negative impact of family-blaming theories. Sometimes the results have been disastrous.

Kathryn's daughter Cindy became suicidal during her first year at McGill University. Kathryn flew to Montreal and, overcoming many obstacles from an uncooperative hospital, she was able to bring her back to Vancouver.

Over the next five years, Cindy, a previously very well-adjusted and extremely competent young woman, made numerous serious suicide attempts. Kathryn tried, unsuccessfully, to talk to the psychiatrists that Cindy saw during the hospitalizations that followed these attempts and even had Cindy's permission to do this since they managed to keep their strong relationship intact during these chaotic years.

Kathryn had begun keeping careful notes of the patterns of the extreme highs and lows that Cindy experienced and tried to get staff to consider a diagnosis of bipolar disorder, especially since Cindy's biological father was severely bipolar. Because Cindy's self-harm included cutting, an easy but incorrect diagnosis of a borderline personality disorder was made.

Finally, after five years, during one hospitalization an open-minded staff member was very interested in hearing from Kathryn, and connected her and Cindy to a widely experienced psychiatrist who quickly saw the bipolar disorder. The resulting change in treatment meant that after five horrific years, Cindy was able to go back to school and realize her inherent potential to become a successful student.

Most of the women in these groups are fortunate and their children, often with skilful assistance from the mothers, have become able to accept, understand and manage their disorders. Of course, when relapses occur, insight often vanishes and situations can quickly escalate out of control despite the best efforts of families.

Too often parents have to deal with misguided mental health professionals who block their involvement. Lack of adequate training in serious mental illnesses sometimes leads workers to pursue dangerous strategies. Even though research consistently shows that family involvement saves the health system money, the involvement of families is undermined even though their efforts often keep their ill family members on medications and connected to rehabilitation programs.

Some mental health professionals apply inappropriate concerns about separation and individuation. Molly's family physician, who'd limited her interactions with us, thought it made sense to ask someone in full-blown mania what dose of medication she'd like to be on. All of the mothers I know want their sons and daughters to live full, independent lives. At the same time, they know that their unusual involvement with their adult children may be very necessary for a long time to help this happen.

Some of these women, like me, have quit or drastically reduced their working lives in order to best assist their ill children to get better. There are basically no respite services available beyond those that we arrange and finance ourselves. The single mothers I've met are often extraordinarily stressed and struggling to meet demands that are impossible.

I feel all of these women have been ignored by leading feminists; in looking over conference programs, I see that some of these powerful women are continuing to relate to issues of serious mental illnesses in the ways that I remember from the 1970s. At that point, feminism helped women respond to patriarchal assumptions in psychotherapy that pathologized the justified discontent that women had from living in an unequal society.

I see a lot of evidence that these feminist perspectives have continued to dominate the research agenda of some female scholars. I can't find any evidence of feminist thinkers who have looked at the circumstances of women who are choosing to take on the enormous responsibilities of caring for their adult children who suffer from serious mental illnesses. I don't see articles written about the undermining of these women's efforts, an undermining that probably rests on the mother-blaming theories that continue to have power.

There's one source of stress that is difficult for the moms to discuss outside of these groups. Ironically, there is often abuse occurring in these households but the parents aren't the perpetrators.

Ill people, who under normal circumstances are very gentle and reasonable, can become desperately angry and volatile when they are in the throes of their illnesses. Because neutral stimuli often begin being processed in the fear centres of the brain, unwell people can become very paranoid; if they are involved with their families, then family members often become the villains in their delusional thinking.

How easy it has been for poorly educated professionals to assume that the accusations made while ill must be revealing deep truths instead of completely disordered thinking. These moms sometimes have to make difficult decisions in these situations in order to protect younger children in the household; they may want their ill child to continue to live at home but cannot do this because of inadequate supports.

Mental health support workers are paid to visit and assist consumers who live in supported housing but not those who are living at home. This lack of services only ends up costing the government more money. It's not just the less well supported consumers whose health deteriorates; research is demonstrating the detrimental impact on the health of people who are full-time care-givers.

New Ways to Break

Spring 2003-Summer 2004

We are scheduled to see Jane Garland again before our next appointment with Bill. Jane has been a very helpful consultant over the previous year, encouraging our connection to the St. Paul's Team and to Menninger's. All consultants had advised Dr. Z to keep raising the Olanzapine but none of the nine psychiatrists who knew about Molly being on both drugs had warned us of the nature of their interaction. Maybe they each assumed Dr. Z was taking this apparently well known drug interaction into account. Jane does not pass the buck, although it has rarely been in her hands. She writes up the oversight in her report.

When we see Jane, we have an even more urgent problem to report. Though Molly is clearly no longer psychotic, she has developed strange new behaviours. She knows that they aren't rational so this isn't psychosis. I watched her notice a tiny bit of paint chipped off the kitchen door frame. She mentioned it and then wondered if someone could have eaten it by mistake and then wondered if she'd eaten it and began to obsess about this bizarre possibility.

These strange fixations have expanded and they mostly have to do with worrying about her health. She's become hyperaware of her own heartbeat and constantly wonders if something is wrong with it. She's become relentlessly concerned about germs and is washing her hands several times each hour. Just as I had explained the initial angry outbursts of her mania three years earlier by honouring her newfound assertiveness, I normalize these behaviours. I assume she is realizing how ill she's been and doesn't trust her body yet.

Jane asks me what I know about the anxiety disorder called obsessive compulsive disorder. Like with bipolar disorder and schizophrenia, I realize that whatever I thought I knew is wrong. Didn't Freud think excessive hand-washing related to repressive childhoods full of guilt-inducing shaming?

These new behaviours have nothing in common with the bits of memory I have about his interpretations. Jane says that often people coming out of a severe psychosis go on to develop OCD and recommends Jeffrey Schwartz's book *Brainlock* which explains the neurophysiology of this disorder and successful ways to treat it. The best treatments involve using both antidepressants and cognitive behavioural therapy (CBT) to get the brain unstuck from the repeating neural loop which plagues sufferers of this disorder.

The CBT techniques train people to monitor their thinking patterns and master strategies which free their thoughts from their obsessive patterns. People learn how to avoid performing the compulsive acts which have grown out of their irrational obsessions.

I also learn that OCD can be triggered by strep infections which Molly hasn't had. Unfortunately, a new catalyst has emerged: high doses of atypical anti-psychotics like Olanzapine can create OCD. Strangely, low doses of these same drugs are effectively used to treat the disorder. Anti-depressants are the major medication that can help; Molly has not been exposed to them since her devastating dose of Paxil. Apparently, any of the anti-depressants, both the newer SSRI's and the older tricyclics, can trigger mania in people with bipolar disorder. We'll have to find another solution.

Bill decides to begin slowly lowering Molly's 60 mg dose of Olanzapine. Her psychotic symptoms have not recurred and people usually require a much lower dose of an antipsychotic for maintenance. We hope the lowering of Olanzapine can keep her psychosis away, maintain her mood stability, and free her from the ever growing hold the OCD is having over her life.

Something new and troubling begins to happen. From the earliest stages of Molly's illness, her basic movement abilities have been impacted. Even before she had her psychotic break, her gait had become awkward; the glorious ease and grace that she'd had as a younger child when she moved had disappeared. It was as if the growing tumult of her mind had seized even her instinctive ability to walk in a coherent way.

Now, she's developed odd twitches in her left arm and a recurring stiffness on her right side. These aren't huge issues to us; she's certainly lived with many worse symptoms than whatever might be happening.

Bill's face darkens as I mention these problems at our next appointment. We've seen him several times since her dramatic emergence from psychosis and the sessions have had a jubilant tone. He's told us how grim the predictions from the St. Paul's Refractory Team had been and is eager to tell them that they all got it wrong. I love his humility. It's a quality I keep finding in the best practitioners.

He also tells us how hopeful Molly's prognosis has become. Molly's sense of humour has returned and her characteristic empathy for the feelings of others is readily apparent. Both of these qualities, he explains, are very key predictors of future recovery.

But, today, he's very sombre as he asks Molly to walk in a straight line and perform other simple motor tasks. Then he begins telling us about tardive dyskinesia. I am barely listening. This is a disorder I do know about from my earlier training and work in psychiatric institutions.

People who spent years on the traditional antipsychotics have ended up with these gruesome side effects. Twitches and jerks can rock their whole body; their tongues begin drooping uncontrollably out of their mouths. Neither of us explains to Molly that these symptoms aren't usually reversible. She's not especially worried about the strange movements; all of her worrying has been absorbed by the growing intensity of her OCD.

One of the great benefits of the newer atypical antipsychotics had been that they don't cause tardive dyskinesia. This seemed to be the case when they came on the market and when they were prescribed at the small doses that had been used in clinical trials. Time has shown that each of them is also able to trigger this gruelling side effect.

Bill explains that the drugs not only trigger the disorder but, at high doses, mask its presence. It's only because we are lowering her dose of Olanzapine that the presence of tardive dyskinesia has been revealed. There seems to be a small chance that it could go away but as I begin to look in the literature this doesn't seem likely. In the months to come, the quantity of twitches and jerks increases; Bill tells me it's the worst case of tardive dyskinesia he's ever seen in a young person.

There is one side effect of medications that is having a positive impact. Although Molly only spent a few weeks on Clozapine, the feeling of choking on saliva and any food in her mouth has continued to bother her. She refuses to eat any solid food and will only drink Boost and tomato soup. I supplement this inadequate diet with vitamins and wonder if this feeling will ever leave her.

It takes five months before she feels ready to eat solid food again. Molly, like many people, has had a huge weight gain on Olanzapine. By June, the fifty pounds that she'd gained have disappeared and she is back to a size 5 and seeing her, in a moment of stillness, can still evoke images of what she was before nature betrayed her.

Molly looks lovely when, one night in June, Naomi helps her get ready for a performance of the staged reading of the winning script from the *This Is a Spoon One-Act Playwriting Contest*.

The *Eye of the Storm* is masterful; the author of the winning script has been revealed to be Peter Zednik. He's a well-known playwright/director connected to Vancouver's internationally successful Green Thumb Theatre. The main character, a teenage girl who is developing schizophrenia, is a very appealing and likable character. Any consumers (of mental health services) in the audience will feel that their experiences are being presented in a compassionate light. Parents, too, will feel affirmed by the rattled, but caring mother who is trying to manage an impossible situation.

Up to now, any depiction I've ever seen of the parents of someone with schizophrenia shows them to be selfish, twisted evildoers, whose abusive behaviours have doomed their children to tormented lives. The mom in this play is like the mothers I've been meeting – devoted and desperate.

Molly still hasn't been around large groups of people and gets overwhelmed fairly easily. I seat the girls early so that the cramped space of Playwrights Theatre Centre doesn't crowd her, even if the event pulls in the audience I'm hoping for. PTC has been pushing for a one - night only performance although we have a contract for me to pay for two evenings. I think they're fearful that the array of top Vancouver actors they've assembled will be performing for empty seats. It's a legitimate worry; several readings of new plays I've attended in this intimate theatre drew less than twenty people.

I've begun assembling an email list of families I've been meeting who have a mentally ill child and encouraged them to come to the play. Deanna has also sent word out to mental health staff in the Vancouver system. It's a great cheap professional development opportunity.

I'm unsure how many mental health staff members have had any exposure to presentations about serious mental illnesses that don't make the parents be culprits. I've put together the kind of panel I've wanted to see – a consumer of mental health services, a psychiatrist and another mental health professional who works with people with serious mental illnesses. The moderator of the panel is a theatre professor from UBC with a special interest in representations of mental illness in the arts.

I'm tense as I wait with PTC staff at the ticket counter; some people have made reservations but the 100 seats aren't close to being filled. I've done an interview earlier in the afternoon for the Canadian Broadcasting Corporation (CBC) about the event but was thrown when the interviewer asked me an unexpectedly detailed personal question about my daughter's illness.

I'd worked for CBC for three years, long before Molly was born, as a writer/broadcaster about dance events. The reviews I did were usually taped and I'd listen to them when they aired, looking for clues about how to make them more effective. This interview was live and I'm glad I didn't have to listen later to the sound of my voice trembling as I stumbled through a sentence about Molly being better. I knew enough not to begin to describe all of the limitations she still has and the horrors of her current struggles with tardive dyskinesia and OCD. These aren't hellish truths I could begin to discuss in smooth conversational tones; they are tearing me apart.

By 7:30, people are beginning to arrive for 8 pm and the staff is looking less anxious. I know most of the people who are coming; they are the parents I've been meeting. Some arrive with their children but the children of others are much too ill to sit through a performance or aren't even able to understand that they have an illness.

Old friends are also appearing, including many people who haven't approached us to ask about what's been happening during these two years; they now have a tangible way of showing support about a situation that must have been awkward for them to respond to.

By 7:55, the staff is looking anxious again; the house is full and people are still arriving. They find a few more chairs. The performance sells out on both evenings and I'm hoping that people in the theatre community can realize that there is an eager market for work that explores the lived experiences of real people struggling with serious mental illnesses.

The performance is electric. The actors realize they're performing for an intensely focused audience who are completely present as each moment unfolds. I feel that consumers and family members are seeing a version of their own agonizing stories given back to them with the artistic lens they've been denied. The loud applause lasts a long time; the audience doesn't want to let go of the experience they've been having. By the time people are milling during the intermission and exploring the display I've asked the BCSS to set-up, the atmosphere is celebratory.

I see Molly enveloped by the understanding and friendly groups I've yearned for her to have access to. Even strangers are talking to each other. It's as if people are suddenly proud to be a part of this besieged community of people dealing with mental illnesses.

Everyone settles quickly as the panel presentations begin. People who know little about these illnesses are given an easily understood overview. Then Peter Zednik explains his research process. He proceeded in such a reasonable way to write a dramatic script based on both scientific data and experiences of real people. Why had this been so difficult to ask for in the PTC website? The audience is full of comments and questions when the houselights go up.

The most riveting comment of the two evenings comes from someone who will, years later, become a friend of Molly's. He's arrived with his large family and he stands up slowly to make his comment. Part of what's been terrible about having schizophrenia, he says, is that he hasn't been able to explain to his family what his illness has been like; now, they understand, and they can feel closer to him.

His family, like many others, wants to linger as the PTC staff cleans up afterwards. I'm beginning to see what healing there might be in events where isolated families and consumers can be in an environment together, where the life altering circumstances the illnesses bring can be examined in knowledgeable, cooperative and hopeful ways.

As I finish packing up, I notice that I am happy. Maybe there is a way that I can stop feeling so tormented by what has happened and is happening to Molly. In some way, my own well-being is linked to experiencing the kind of community I had access to for these two nights.

Our social lives have changed dramatically since the onset of Molly's illness. We used to regularly have friends over for dinner but that became impossible when life began to be so unpredictable. There's no way to know if a crisis might arise. We also began to drop friendships with people who weren't interested in or couldn't understand what was happening with Molly. And we became much closer to people who wanted to learn and to help.

Now that so many people we know arrived to be part of the PTC evenings, we feel like our situation doesn't require as much explanation. We begin to have people over for dinner again, confident that we and they can adapt to whatever troubling events might occur.

I still want to get a better grasp on the broader issues. Menninger staff had emphasized the importance of the National Alliance for the Mentally Ill (NAMI). Many of the founding members, like Dr. E. Fuller Torrey, had relatives with schizophrenia or bipolar disorder. I know that thousands of people go to their annual conferences and I decide to go right after the PTC project ends. The 2003 summer conference is in Minneapolis and it's an unexpected bonus to find that some other Canadians have also come.

We seek each other out, trying to compare the situations for families and consumers in our different provinces. Walking through the halls of the conference hotel is affirming and also painful. There are many elderly parents who are accompanied by their middle-aged children who show the strains of lives filled with mental illnesses. Is this the future we are facing with Molly?

The American families' problems are much worse than the situations of Canadians because we have socialized medicine. Even people who have health insurance are struggling financially. People have not received parity from their insurance companies for mental illnesses; it will still be several years before the US Congress will pass legislation forcing these companies to respond to mental illnesses with the same degree of service as other physical illnesses.

I try to estimate what Molly's illness has cost the government; the hundreds of thousands of dollars that I add up help me understand why many people in the US are saying these illnesses have bankrupted them.

Despite the economic hardships, American families seem to have become better organized through their local NAMI chapters. State caucuses meet to train members on how to advocate on local, state and national levels for changes they want. The excellent Family to Family psychoeducation course that I've just finished taking through the BCSS was developed by NAMI's Joyce Burland and is being taught by NAMI branches across the US and around the world.

I'd been hearing that a BRIDGES course is becoming available in Vancouver; BRIDGES, too, was developed by NAMI and provides a comprehensive psychoeducation course taught by consumers for consumers. If people really understand their illnesses, they will be much more able to accept and manage them. I hope Molly can be involved in this.

One of the most exciting parts of the conference is an annual event called *Ask the Psychiatrist*. Panels of psychiatrists steeped in the clinical and research issues of their specialties gather in rooms and audiences ask them questions. In the schizophrenia session, I hear questions about clinical trials of medications to deal with the cognitive deficits that often accompany schizophrenia.

This is the first time that I'm hearing about predictable cognitive losses associated with schizophrenia even after psychosis has been brought under control. The audience is very familiar with problems with concentration, sustained focus, working memory, sequencing and problem solving skills. These are all phenomena I've been seeing in Molly but haven't understood that they might be ongoing problems.

Various research studies are investigating cognitive remediation strategies. It looks as though people who can actually afford great care for their family member may have access to all kinds of programs that I haven't heard about in Canada. Well planned therapeutic communities have been established in idyllic rural areas for people who can spend $60,000 a year getting intensive care in a residential setting.

The conference leaves me much more oriented to a bigger picture about the issues facing people with serious mental illnesses and their families. I'm inspired by the power of a conference like this to strengthen, educate, and mobilize families in new ways. Why doesn't some version of this kind of conference exist in Vancouver?

My task when I return is to persuade Hamber House to keep Molly for one more year. The Coordinator has decided it's time for her to move on to UBC's Schizophrenia Rehabilitation Day Program. I know that for the next year the safest, most nurturing environment will be Hamber House.

The UBC program has a lot of much older participants and has also had a problem with some participants being involved with heroin. Hamber House has provided protection from the problems that come along with older clients. Also, now that Molly is no longer psychotic, she needs to keep trying to work on her basic education. The Day Program, unlike Hamber House, doesn't have a teacher. As well, Molly has a deep bond with Deanna, her counsellor, who knows her well and is skilled in working with CBT.

Finally we realize that, since the Vancouver School Board works with students until their 19th birthday, we can argue that the district is responsible for Molly's education all through the fall when she'll still be 18; Hamber House is the only school that can possibly accommodate her unique learning needs.

As it becomes evident that we are going to persist in advocating for what we believe is best, Molly gets permission to stay. This plan also means that the following year she'll be able to attend the Day Program for a year. She's so fragile and so limited that a non-sheltered environment would be impossible for her to manage. We have no idea what she'll be able to do when her year at the Day Program ends.

All through the summer and the fall, Bill monitors the lowering of Olanzapine. Molly's psychosis isn't returning but her tardive dyskinesia and OCD get worse. When we try to go below 15 mg. of Olanzapine, Molly's manic behaviour begins to return. By the fall, we've added Valproate; this could help maintain her mood stability which is slipping away as the Olanzapine is reduced.

It doesn't work and we need to introduce another atypical antipsychotic, Seroquel, which might have less risk for exacerbating tardive dyskinesia. Bill is able to schedule a planned admission to UBC Hospital in January 2004 where the rest of the Olanzapine can be withdrawn in a protected environment while the raising of the level of Seroquel can be closely monitored.

As is often the case, being in a new environment temporarily relieves a lot of Molly's OCD. We've talked through this admission to UBC Hospital with Molly and she's been supportive of the plan. The re-emergence of her manic symptoms has frightened her. She's become increasingly agitated and irrational. The painful OCD symptoms have become harder for her to endure and she's felt suicidal. Her quick flips into rage have also reappeared and when she calms down she is as troubled by her behaviour as we are; she hates being so out of control.

After Molly gets used to the hospital, she's eager for company; she is accustomed to having ready access to people. She's tried many times to engage the nurses who, when not giving medications, are usually gathered in their station.

Within a couple of days, they've told her that she must stop coming to the nurses' station to talk with them. Since I often overhear them socializing, I'm perplexed about what model of care is being used. Maybe their job really is limited to administering and charting medical procedures. They even seem annoyed when I visit and need to interrupt them to ask a question.

I'm especially troubled by the situation of a couple of young guys on the unit who are emerging from psychotic states and who don't have visitors. Patients' contacts with their psychiatrists are understandably brief and people seem left to their own devices to come to terms with what has been happening to them.

There is not much to do in the hospital and soon we decide to supplement our visits and the visits of our friends, by having the support workers we hire do activities with Molly. They go for walks and even use the UBC gym to workout. They play games and watch videos. Her spirits are especially good for the first week when she's getting a reprieve from her OCD.

We feel that we have come a long way in understanding how to successfully manage a hospital stay. We also realize that this is the first time in almost three years that we've been in our home without having our caregiving responsibilities dominating our days.

We feel hopeful about the possibilities for treating Molly's OCD now that she will have the powerful stabilizing action of Seroquel in place. The literature on treating OCD successfully with SSRI's is exciting. We will still first try one more anticonvulsant mood stabilizer, Lamotrigine, since it is less risky. Experiencing Molly almost free of her OCD for the first week of her hospital stay is very encouraging. Her mental clarity and abilities are waiting to emerge and be rebuilt once the OCD can be managed.

We are so confident that we begin to consider a ten - day trip to France when my summer vacation starts at the end of June. Peter's work with his UBC research projects has gone well but he's been limited in his connections to European colleagues because he hasn't wanted to leave me alone to cope with such unstable situations. He's been asked to be a keynote speaker at a conference in Lyon and we decide to assume this might be possible. The worst case scenario is that I'll have to stay behind.

Molly's 1200 mg dose of Seroquel should keep her stable when she comes home from the hospital; usual doses are between 400 and 800 mg. However, she's returned from the hospital in rough shape. By the second week in the hospital her vacation from OCD had faded and all kinds of objects in her room were a source of worry and she was spending long periods of time washing her hands. Nobody on the unit seemed prepared to re-enforce the Cognitive Behavioural Therapy techniques she'd been learning over the previous year that could sometimes help her get over the worst moments of her OCD.

When she gets home, her old OCD issues quickly return within a few days. She is again frightened of germs, of pencils, of scissors, and of glass thinking that she could somehow ingest and be injured by each of these. One afternoon she is especially distraught by the oppressiveness of her OCD. She just wants to die, she says, and runs to the kitchen picking up the largest knife, the one that has terrified her the most.

I grab her wrist to get it away from her but her grip is too strong. We fall to the floor and as I manage to pin her arms to the ground, she and I are both sobbing. Is this our new future?

Bill is out of town but the Hamber House psychiatrist suggests raising the Seroquel up to 1400 mg. and it works. She becomes calmer and more able to battle the persistent OCD. Maybe the Lamotrigine we soon add to fight the OCD is also helping her feel more balanced. It's just one more disappointment when it causes a troubling rash that can be the sign of a more dangerous condition and we have to phase it out.

By late spring we are ready to risk Luvox, an SSRI that is often effective in battling OCD. Molly is moving better; her right arm no longer stiffly juts out to the side and her tongue remains in her mouth. The Luvox begins to work; gradually the OCD relinquishes its terrible hold on her brain, and she's freer to respond more of the time to the world around her. The support workers have trained her to jog and she's going on more walking and bicycling adventures with them to the beaches and forests.

She's learning more in her classes at Hamber House and will be strong enough to manage the transition to the UBC Day Program in September.

Blindsided

Summer 2004

Naomi is ready to move in for ten days as we are about to leave for the trip to France. She's just taken on a new job as an intern at the Holocaust Education Centre and our house is even closer to her work.

Molly's a little unstable from the Luvox but has insight into these fluctuations and works hard to manage these small mood swings herself. She and we are relieved to see the irrational fears of the kitchen fade. She is very proud the day that she can make lunch by herself; we are enthusiastically supportive and try not to think about how many tasks of daily life are still beyond her.

A few days before we leave, Peter sees an ophthalmologist for a problem he's been having with his left eye. It's painful and an antibiotic hasn't cleared up a potential infection. The ophthalmologist sends him out for a CAT scan which reveals a small mass. He's able to quickly get an appointment with Jack Rootman, an outstanding oncological ophthalmologist whom Peter knows.

He'll arrange for a biopsy but lets us know that even if the tumour is cancerous, they can often be treated easily with radiation. Even though Peter has to cancel the trip to France, we are fine with what is happening. We love the expertise we are seeing; unlike treating a very complicated mental illness like Molly's, Peter's small tumour is a mild inconvenience. Lots of people we know have been treated for cancer. We'll just plan a small getaway for later in the summer.

The biopsy is complicated. There is so much blood in the tumour that rests in his ethmoid sinus cavity that the ear, nose and throat oncologist can't get an adequate batch of cells to examine. Peter will have to be hospitalized and have the blood vessels feeding the tumour cauterized in order to get a sample.

This surgery ends up involving several days in the hospital and Peter reacts badly to the anaesthetic. Naomi and I take turns being with him while his grogginess and nausea slowly fade. It seems to be taking a long time for the surgeon to get the results of the biopsy and I go home to be with a somewhat skittish Molly.

Molly is very close to Peter who devotedly drove her to years of baseball, ringette and soccer practices and games, and tennis lessons. He'd become the major tutor as her difficulties with homework kept expanding. Having him in the hospital for even this minor procedure is making her anxious.

I haven't been home very long when Naomi calls. I can barely recognize her voice and realize she's crying, something she very rarely does. She wants me to come to the hospital right away. The surgeon has returned and she can only report that, "It's bad."

Poor Naomi must have been shocked by the dirtiness of St. Paul's hospital and is unnerved to see her vibrantly fit father lying in a hospital bed. I tell her she can go home and

I'll be right there. We've been such a healthy family, except for Molly's illness, that she just hasn't developed many skills to cope with the usual range of afflictions that are bound to happen.

She's hasn't left St. Paul's when I arrive but she's no longer crying. She's arranging for some kind of procedure and it's several minutes before she's ready to explain the situation. But she doesn't need to explain because the surgeon has returned and seems relieved as he tells me how he's tracked down the problem which he's already described to Peter and Naomi.

It was a complicated diagnosis but he's sure he's right. I smile encouragingly wanting to also marvel at his diagnostic skills and continue smiling and nodding as he says how unusual it is to find a kidney cancer tumour in the head. I wonder if this will mean chemo as well as radiation. Maybe there will have to be some kind of surgery. I keep listening to get the details about what we're supposed to do next since Peter's still pretty tired.

I don't think I understand what I'm hearing.

"Unfortunately, kidney cancer isn't curable. There isn't any chemotherapy for it. Since Peter's tumour is far from his kidneys, the cancer has metastasized and can be anywhere. I'll notify the palliative team to come meet with you tomorrow."

Is he telling us that Peter is dying?

Peter had already heard this and is calm. We are both ready to comfort Naomi but she's figuring out different ways to cope. She's already arranged the hard to schedule screening which will later confirm a silent kidney tumour.

Now she's gotten out paper to make a list of all of her friends' connections with physicians including a well respected palliative care doctor with a lot of experience with cancer.

I'm watching her add to her list, figuring out whom we should see in the BC Cancer Agency, and how she can obtain the quickest appointment. I see her do the things I've been doing for three years in fighting against Molly's illness but, now, I am struck silent. I can't figure out any next steps. Naomi's assuming control and is already arranging to take a leave of absence from her new job by the time we leave the hospital. Naomi's attachment to Peter has always been fierce and death is going to have to fight really hard if it's planning to take her beloved father away from her.

Peter needs to stay in the hospital for a couple of days to recover from the messy biopsy and he's falling asleep as we leave. Naomi's going back to her apartment to research kidney cancer and make contact with the people who can guide us.

I'm evasive with Molly when I get home and close the door to my office. We need help and I call Noah, Peter's brother. It's hard for him to understand me because I'm whispering so Molly can't hear me and my voice keeps breaking. Noah is a professor at the University of Washington and isn't teaching for the summer. He will leave for Vancouver the next day.

My sister, Sally, lives in Washington DC and offers to come but relating to too many people is hard. I e-mail friends with the diagnosis; I don't want anyone to call because it is easier to write about the death sentence that Peter has been given than to make myself say it aloud.

Naomi comes for the evening and our carefully cultivated good spirits sweep Molly along. Peter will be home in a couple of days and even Noah is coming for a visit. If Molly senses any undertones, she's not reacting to them. She's been diligently using CBT to avoid unnecessary worrying.

Unbelievably, Naomi has been able to arrange for an appointment at the BC Cancer Agency for the next day, before Peter even leaves St. Paul's. He's sent by ambulance and we gather in Dr. Chi's office. Dr. Chi confirms the worst; kidney cancer is incurable; nauseating ongoing treatments with Interferon might keep someone alive a little longer; 97% of people die within two years, most within the first year; the tumour in his head has attached to the dura mater of his brain; cancer of the brain will probably soon spread and it's a very difficult way to die.

Peter could have surgeries but they would be palliative; they might buy some more time but the surgery to his head will be especially difficult and he might not survive without brain damage.

Peter is peaceful and Naomi and I struggle to maintain our composure. Peter talks about the fortunate life he's had, his unusually happy and privileged childhood; the joys of our marriage and family; the meaningful career. He feels ready to die without more surgeries.

Naomi and I are determined to support whatever decision he makes but we have a hard time speaking through the sobs we can no longer control. These sounds fill the deadly silence.

Dr Chi listens and then guides us.

"I don't think I've made the situation clear. The surgeries would be palliative but they might give the people who love you the extra time they want with you. "

This is all that it takes.

As soon as someone tells Peter that he should do something for us, he is immediately on board. Dr. Chi will work to schedule the head surgery as soon as possible but because it will require the removal of his left eye and the reconfiguration of his ethmoid sinus cavity and the dura of his brain, it will involve a neurosurgeon, a plastic surgeon, and an ear, nose and throat oncologist; the kidney surgeons will operate later. Dr. Chi is careful to mention that Peter might be disfigured afterwards but not even Peter is concerned. We think we've just bought time and nothing else matters.

The palliative team at St. Paul's meets with us later that afternoon. We decide where in our house we'll be able to put the hospital bed. Molly doesn't need the ping-pong table now that she's able to go out to do more and I'll put in comfortable chairs near the bed for people to visit with Peter.

Life is a ridiculous hell and I'll just navigate narrow pathways of duty before chaos claims us all.

Next on my to-do list is helping Molly understand that her devoted father is dying and that soon our house will be a palliative centre. Peter is spending another night in St. Paul's to mend from the invasive biopsy. In just a few days, he's transformed from a radiantly healthy man to a stooped, weakened figure who's in a wheelchair. Naomi finds out about a rooftop garden at the hospital so that I can bring Molly someplace peaceful. She'll bring in fresh clothes for Peter and have him already sitting in some way that makes the wheelchair less obvious.

Molly is tense and subdued on the ride to the hospital where she's finally going to get to see Peter. She knows he has cancer and will be having surgery. When she asks if he's going to be okay, I pause and try to distract her with the radio. She doesn't ask again about what she doesn't want to know.

The evening sky is still light with a soft blue-grey haze. The rooftop garden isn't being used by anyone else and Naomi has arranged the most beautiful area near blooming planters for us to sit. Molly wraps her arms around Peter and starts talking. She's missed him and can hardly wait for him to come home tomorrow. He's going to be okay, right? She's able to wait quietly during the silence and he tells her that he may not be okay but that she will be, that this peaceful feeling she gets from hugging us can always be there for her, that our love can keep her safe. Peter, Naomi and I have planned and committed to our calm acceptance of the worst news Molly can hear. She breaks into heart-wrenching sobs. We try to keep her safe as we softly surround her with our loving words.

Safe? Safe is up here on the rooftop with our bare souls letting go of everything but our deep loving presence with each other. And we're leaving safety when she and I go back down the stairs and out the hospital door. We make our way through a small group of quiet, bedraggled men smoking next to their shopping carts. Does some version of our own unforeseen circumstances explain how they got here? Who wasn't able to keep them safe?

Peter arrives home the next day; there's a two-week wait for the head surgery and rounds of appointments with specialists before the hospitalization. He's finally recovering his energy from the biopsy and he's set up his watercolours in the backyard. Naomi, on leave from her new job, has brought over her drawing pads. The dogwood tree is completely covered in delicate white flowers and the back deck's ceramic pots are spilling over with blooms eager to be alive.

Molly's volatility on the Luvox is growing but friends are taking her out to do her favourite things and the young women who have been doing support and rehabilitation work with her during these years are rearranging their schedules to be available.

I rarely cook for weeks; people keep dropping off salads, soups, and casseroles. My friends Kitty and Gloria have stocked our fridge and freezer with weeks of meals. Our living room looks like a florist's shop. Peter's generous nature and irrepressible good spirits have always made people in his life appreciate him and now they are trying to help us.

We keep being unjustifiably serene as we inhale the sweetness of July. Except for Molly. The brief flares of breakthrough mania that the Luvox can bring are increasing and lasting longer. Finally, one afternoon, she breaks into an agitated rant and can't be guided back. Bill is out of town as is Dr. R. who is taking over her care in August at the Day Program. I call a psychiatrist friend who says it's safe to stop the Luvox all at once and within a couple of days Molly settles. The OCD finds the vacancy and takes up residence.

Noah returns for the head surgery and he and Naomi wait with Molly when Peter goes into St. Paul's the night before for a procedure that will reduce the blood flow to the tumour site and will leave his left eye blind before it is removed the next day.

The nurses are very supportive and let me wait for him in his room. Peter's a bit sleepy when he returns from this minor surgery but in good humour. Any trace of pettiness between us has evaporated since his diagnosis; we know there's not much time left. We have found something to giggle about when a new nurse comes in to evaluate him.

Her exam is efficient but she's upset when she keeps shining a small flashlight into his left eye and his pupil doesn't respond. Her English skills are pretty good but this unexpected response has thrown her and she leaves before we can explain. She returns with a different flashlight and tries again and we join forces to make her hear the information that's been left off the chart. We console her; his left eye is supposed to be blind now; there's nothing to worry about.

In dealing with the various physicians and the hospital, I feel as though I've tapped into a completely different medical system. When my fifteen year old was out of her mind, I had to pry information out of suspicious - looking professionals. Now that my husband, still a basically competent adult, is groggy at times, people trust me to make all kinds of decisions without showing any kind of Power of Attorney.

Peter's surgical team is an outstanding and highly collaborative group. Like all other Canadians, I'm worried about wait times and when first hearing about the possibility of surgery, I'd thought we should remortgage the house and head to Sloan Kettering. A surgeon explained that even though it's not easy to get non-emergency procedures like knee replacements, people in Vancouver who deal with life-threatening situations receive the best care in the world.

The ENT surgeon contacts me immediately after the surgery. He describes how successful it was, says the margins are good, and he tells me about a way to get into the recovery room. Peter is sleeping peacefully; his abdomen and thigh have been cut open to glean pieces of his own flesh to reform his eye socket and all this wounded skin is concealed beneath the sheet.

His left eye is neatly covered with a soft leathery - looking patch that's been sewed in place with thick, even stitches. I watch him for a while before it dawns on me that the leather is his own skin, part of the harvesting of other parts of his body that's occurred. I know I can't touch his long body that still looks so strong; it feels as though he could just wake up and walk out with the new, nicely designed artwork covering his eye socket. At least he won't have to worry about adjusting to living with disfigurement; he's reconfigured but his long, angular face is still achingly beautiful to me.

When he wakes up hours later, he doesn't just get up and walk away. He is horribly sick from the anaesthetic and all of the torn up pieces of his body, now swollen, are protesting with searing pain. Various pain medication strategies are tried and over the next few days, his most severe agony fades. He spends days in a step-down unit where I've never seen nurses work so hard. They must be understaffed because these women are regularly missing their breaks and even meals in order to deliver the non-stop care their patients require. Naomi, Noah and I trade shifts between being with Peter and helping care for Molly.

I decide to delay the rental of the hospital bed; after nine days in the hospital, Peter wants to be back in our spacious bedroom with the wall of windows and the skylights that open to precious views of days and nights.

His weakened state has led to a delay in the surgery to remove his right kidney and the large, dark, tumour that's attached to it. He doesn't go into UBC Hospital until September when Molly is beginning the Day Program. By now the skilled surgical team understands his difficulty with anaesthesia and responsiveness to certain pain medications. When I visit him after dropping Molly off at the adjacent hospital each morning, he feels good. I again delay the setting up of the death room.

New Ways to be Trapped

Fall 2004 – Fall 2005

I'd seen the patients at Day Program earlier when we'd had an orientation. There are almost twenty guys and three girls counting Molly. Most of the patients look pretty ill; many have the remote, flattened affect and the heavy sluggishness that either the negative symptoms are producing or that are occurring before the best dosages of medications are discovered.

I learn from a couple of parents whose children had participated in the program that the rehabilitation program is far from ideal. There seems to be about six weeks of programming that is then repeated. No one on staff seems to do the intense Cognitive Behavioural Therapy techniques that Deanna had taught Molly and that had finally, with the help of the Luvox, begun to enable her to manage her OCD.

The Anxiety Disorders Clinic which is in the same building specializes in CBT but won't take patients with schizophrenia no matter how well their psychotic symptoms are controlled. I only mention cognitive remediation techniques once because no one seems to be aware of the existence of these programs which have expanded in the US.

I am very grateful for Molly to have access to this daily program. I know many people are able to stay for a year and I'm hoping that Molly will be allowed this privilege. She needs to be with other young people who are adjusting to the same disorders; it's not clear if she'll ever be able to be in a non-sheltered learning environment again. There are groups she could benefit from including weekly sessions on goal-planning, medications, cooking, psychoeducation, relaxation and fitness.

Dr. R has prescribed Clonazepam to reduce some of the anxiety that the return of her OCD is producing. Understandably, he wants to wait and observe her before deciding next steps. I've been scared before of having Molly use Ativan or Clonazepam because of the risk of addiction to benzodiazepines but I am learning that when people, like Molly, really need them then the risk of addiction is greatly reduced. Later in the fall, Dr. R. decides to prescribe Anafranil, a tricyclic antidepressant that was the first one to receive FDA approval to treat OCD. This sounds like a good choice.

We know that it can take weeks and even months for medications to begin to show how effective they can be. All fall Molly's OCD worsens; her hands are red and raw from the excessive washing that takes long periods of time away from the group activities and it takes her a long time to walk anywhere outside because she feels compelled to look at the bottom of her shoes after every few steps.

The Day Program has a policy where each client has an individual staff member for one-to-one sessions each week. I'm glad that Molly gets this time even though she doesn't receive the CBT that I know she needs. Many of the patients have OCD since it often emerges following a serious psychotic break and can be induced by large doses of antipsychotics. I'm not sure what methods, if any, are being used to treat the OCD besides medication and education about the disorder.

I've shared with Molly what I've learned from my growing library of materials about OCD and she knows just which parts of her brain get stuck when it's occurring. She remembers the techniques Deanna trained her in, but, without re-enforcement, they seem to be slipping from her grasp.

I'm initially excited when Molly tells me they've finally begun to study OCD. She then describes the film they've been shown, with people wearing clothing styles from twenty years previously when the film was probably made.

The film explains how strict, anxiety-producing behaviours of parents in early childhood lead to the development of the disorder. I can hardly believe this kind of film would be shown but when I check with former staff members, they remember it.

I don't think this Freudian way of understanding OCD has had any credibility in mainstream psychiatry for years. A recently produced and superb Canadian documentary on OCD has been repeatedly aired on the Knowledge Network and I know copies of it have been made available to the Day Program.

Why would they show something like this which will only undermine the tenuous relationship that many patients may have with their families? I e-mail the one staff member whose contact info I have about the issue but am told it's up to each staff member who shows a video to select the one they like best.

Molly only sees Dr. R. on a regular basis in the medication group on Fridays where he assesses participants to determine any needed changes. I am astonished at this policy; shouldn't everyone get at least an occasional private session with the psychiatrist who prescribes their medications? I know Molly is uncomfortable discussing her OCD symptoms in a group which is probably why there's been no change from the Anafranil; this drug is proving to be worse than useless since it's accompanied by uncomfortable physical side effects.

Molly's young and pleasant primary worker goes on leave and we're able to get Dr. R. to take her on as one of his one-to-one clients. Many people have benefitted from Dr. R's work through the years; we know that he's been very effective in helping many young adults begin to understand that they have an illness and need treatment.

We hope that Molly will also now finally get the help she needs. The OCD has grown in its intensity all fall and now in winter we think Molly's ready to try an SSRI again. Dr. R. wants to wait now that he's seeing her alone on a weekly basis. I appreciate that it's hard to return a phone call to discuss the problem with medication and during the next few months he does return a couple of phone calls.

Peter is well enough to get involved and stunned when his call is never returned. I've learned that I can send an e-mail to Dr. R. by way of the secretary who works several days a week. By now I've joined the OCD Foundation in the US, and have done much more research; I know an attempt to reintroduce an SSRI is warranted.

By spring I send copies of research articles justifying this request to Dr. R.'s secretary for her to forward. I do get a return call; Dr. R. is pleased with Molly's progress in the program. He thinks she's doing well and has made great improvements. Maybe it's hard to assess her since the 9 am arrival time means that she's either late and has to sit out sessions or that she falls asleep during groups.

I always wonder if the frantic behaviour he saw when he was discharging her from UBC Hospital the year before is his baseline for her. Maybe he thinks she was upset because she was coming home. He hadn't seen the agitation erupt when the head nurse, in a stern effort to get Molly to hurry up for her discharge appointment with Dr. R., opened her door while she was very slowly dressing.

Since I believe that my late-afternoon naps in Veronica's empty office led her to make wildly inaccurate conclusions, I'm concerned about and wary of the data people use to form their opinions.

I finally ask Molly specifics about her sessions with him; she reports that she just says "fine" when he asks her how she's doing and he always hurries to congratulate her on all of her progress before ending their brief visits.

I'm flabbergasted since she's very open about discussing her relentless struggles with OCD with her support workers and with us. Surely other staff who see her more must have some inkling of how ill she's become. Is there some system where they report observations to him? Do they even know about the problem since most of the OCD behaviours occur just out of their sight?

129

We decide to be as direct as possible in leaving a phone message for Dr. R. Molly spends over half of her waking hours caught in the grip of OCD and we and she want to reintroduce an SSRI. Eventually, he does return the call but refuses to write the prescription.

In our conversation I begin to wonder if he might see me as part of Molly's problem; anxiety disorders can be exacerbated by anxious parents but he doesn't know that anxiety has very rarely been a problem for me. Maybe he thinks my half dozen efforts to contact him since she's been in Day Program have been excessive.

I remember his troubling sessions on EE in the psychoeducation programs. Maybe he's someone who imagines that if patients don't get well, undermining parents must be lurking in the background. But mostly I think about how, even after everything we've learned about managing Molly's disorder, we've allowed ourselves to become trapped again.

We consider approaching Molly's helpful personal physician for a prescription but think this would put her in a difficult position since Molly is being actively treated by a psychiatrist. As well, we are very fearful of doing anything to alienate the staff since Molly could easily be told that it's time for her to move on out of the program. And there's nowhere else to go.

Molly's OCD continues to grow; by the end of the summer it occupies 90% of her waking hours. Her year is up at the Day Program and I'm hoping that she'll enter Vancouver Community College's self-paced GED program.

In order to gain admission, she has to achieve certain

minimal scores on assessment tests that VCC gives incoming students. Having had no educational input at the Day Program, it's doubtful that she'll pass. I get copies of the GED curriculum and hire tutors to prepare her for the exams. Though she's constantly distracted by her OCD, she wants to persevere. With a lot of help, she's able to qualify.

The plan is for her to drop in to the GED program four afternoons a week; its tremendous flexibility is ideal for us in trying to make this enormous adjustment work. Day Program is even adapting and providing the transition time many clients need. Molly will be able to attend on Fridays and thus continue to have contact with other young adults battling illnesses.

The Day Program has been great about encouraging people to socialize with each other on the weekends and this is beginning to happen for Molly. But because many of the participants are still fairly ill, the predictable chaotic situations arise. Several times Molly is stranded in places when she thinks she's meeting up with someone. Although Molly says that a lot of her new friends live with their families, I don't know these parents.

I had hoped to be able to again take the family education course because some of these parents would probably be in it, but there hasn't been room. And then I'd begun asking if the staff could help arrange one evening when families and significant others could meet. Another parent and I offer to do all of the organizing of food, a space, and anything else that might ease the work for staff.

We really just need them to get word out to these families one time and then we can figure out the rest. I'm imagining that a lot of these families, like us, realize we could provide much better support to our unstable children during the stressful misadventures that occur, if we knew each other. Hamber House had had monthly meetings with families that provided this kind of much appreciated opportunity to build more layers of support.

Over two years, I will ask staff for this kind of evening five times and I'm never told the reasoning behind the decision to not facilitate this creation of a community of families. Gradually, through our children, many of us will form this valuable network; we like it and our sons and daughters definitely benefit from the broader community of support that develops.

Getting New Chances

Fall 2005 – Spring 2009

While Molly was still at Hamber House, I'd begun working on a committee with Deborah Simpson, Barbara Forster-Rickard and Vancouver Community College staff to consider setting up a GED program especially for consumers. We had been able to organize a very successful open house for mental health clients and VCC staff to explain the programs they already have that might interest consumers.

The staff is surprised at the large turnout that our efforts to advertise the event have produced. After the explanation of the programs, Deborah, Barbara and I have planned to engage the audience in a brainstorming session about what kinds of supports and accommodations could make success at school more possible for them.

We know the plan is risky; this kind of audience is notoriously quiet and passive. There are painfully few hands that reach up in the beginning as we document all of their thoughts on a large blackboard. But then an astounding energy builds. This might be the first time anyone has ever asked some of these people what they need and want in order to make it possible for them to continue their education, and they have a lot of very useful ideas.

Staff are interested to hear about the medication hangovers that many people have in the mornings which make afternoon classes much more appropriate. The consumers want staff to understand that they might have bad days or weeks and they don't want to be thrown out of programs if they can't attend for a while. The staff are extremely attentive and responsive and the clients learn about a lot of possible programs at VCC that could work for them. Besides the drop-in GED program, there are self-paced secondary completion classes where they can often have one-to-one instruction. The Disability Counselling Office makes clear that they are ready to provide a lot of support to students.

The flexibility with arrival times for the GED and self-paced programs is perfectly suited to this population. I'm not sure what the thinking was behind the Day Program's insistence on prompt arrival for 9 am morning sessions and dismissal at 2 pm on most days. The key learning times for most consumers I've met are afternoons.

The Open House is enthusiastically received and even staff from the Vancouver School Board's Adult Basic Education Programs have attended. They say they have never had a workshop on working with this population and that often students with mental illnesses who enrol in their programs drop out. Isn't this a topic that Special Education Programs in Faculties of Education should be thinking about? UBC's Faculty of Education has positions that are devoted to researching the needs of people with much rarer conditions like autism and visual and auditory impairments. People with these conditions are very deserving of focused attention but why is this huge population of people living with mental illnesses ignored?

A special GED program for consumers could be a bridge for people who've lost their abilities to operate in mainstream society to try to continue their education; we've heard about this kind of program operating at Toronto's Centre for Addiction and Mental Health. VCMHSs resourceful Kim Calsaferri has made funding available for a pilot project and the GED staff are eager but VCC doesn't have funds to invest. VCC has begun to focus on further developing their career and university transfer programs.

The neglected population to which Molly and hundreds of young adults like her in Vancouver belong aren't a priority. In years to come, I will learn more about the enormous toll on the national economy of poorly managed mental illnesses. Why aren't the inexpensive steps that will save the country so much money later being taken all along the way? People who are given appropriate opportunities to rebuild their lives are much less likely to end up in prisons or homeless on the street with ambulances arriving daily to deal with their drug overdoses.

In September, 2005, Molly wants to first just see the small renovated brick building downtown which houses the GED program. On our initial visit we briefly look at the rooms which are comfortable and orderly; she tentatively agrees to a second visit to meet the coordinators and some of the instructors. I can see how frightened she is of trying to do anything academic, even in this small-scale education centre which is attractive and welcoming. This will be the first time in four years that she will be in an environment that isn't designed to deal with people with the most severe mental illnesses.

Seeing how ambivalent Molly is about enrolling in the GED program, I try to think of everything that could make things less overwhelming for her. I've met with the Disabilities Counsellor at the main campus and provided a copy of the Representation Agreement which Molly signed the previous year. This allows us to be involved, whenever necessary, in all aspects of her healthcare, education and finances.

The Counselling Department and the GED staff look relieved when I supply this document; they wouldn't be able to talk with me without it and they can see how many difficulties Molly is going to have. Some of the dedicated staff will tell me a year and a half later, when Molly passes her GED exams, that they'd initially believed she'd never be ready to take them but hoped she could learn useful things by attending the program.

She had so few skills and so many difficulties interfering with her ability to learn. The Head of the Disabilities Counselling Services is eager to make this giant experiment work for Molly and for Brittany who is also going to enter the program. She arranges to drive across the city from the main VCC campus once a week to have lunch with the girls and find ways to support them.

By mid-September, we have switched back to seeing Bill MacEwan. I arrive at the first appointment armed with the research articles justifying a trial of Zoloft. I'd forgotten what it had been like to be in a collaborative relationship with a psychiatrist. As Bill hears about what's happened over the previous year with Molly's OCD, he looks sad. Her recovery had looked as though it could go well and, even though she's not had a psychotic break in the previous year, she is clearly stunted. The redevelopment of her abilities to manage in the world has stalled. He thinks it's a great idea to try Zoloft.

Within a month, Molly's OCD no longer occupies 90% of her consciousness; instead, 90% of her consciousness is now free to rediscover what else she can make of her life. Was there some way that I didn't consider that I could have gotten this prescription in the previous year?

The best part of the preceding twelve months has been that Peter has not died. In fact, all traces of his cancer appear to be gone. His dedicated family doctor, who has offered on-call care all year, has explained that sometimes when the major tumours are removed, the rogue cancer cells that have spread elsewhere die off.

We know the cancer can reappear at any time but Peter has experienced a phenomenal recovery. He's returning full-time to his job at UBC and to all of the projects that his Canada Research Chair entails. I decide to assume he's not dying and that I'll arrange some version of coping if circumstances change. I'm painfully certain that I wouldn't have the emotional stamina to be able to offer Molly the assistance I do without all of the tender support Peter gives me. And I don't want to confront these deficits if I don't have to.

Even though Molly's OCD is so much better, the adjustment to the GED program is very hard. Her progress in rebuilding her attention span and her basic abilities to learn is extremely slow. Her working memory, short-term memory and ability to sequence in planning any task have been badly impacted. Also, she doesn't know how to relate to the students around her or to explain what she's been doing with her life for the past four years. Fortunately, the Day Program has allowed her to connect to a group of other young adults who understand each other's conditions very well. Now that her OCD is under control, she can be much more actively involved in the social events they plan.

A group of people from Day Program and their friends begin to get together to play poker at the condo where one of the guys lives with his father. I view this as terrific from all angles; the card game uses math skills, there's lots of socializing, and they even go out to clubs in the city afterwards. I'm not very concerned when Molly mentions that some of the people drink alcohol. Molly is well aware that the last time she drank, she became psychotic for two years and she has been adamant in considering herself a non-drinker.

As Molly recovers from her two years of hellish OCD, settles into her routine with the GED classes, and builds an expanded social network, life in our house is peaceful again. I return to teaching part time and Peter has picked up his teaching and research load at UBC. We relax, released from the hyper vigilance of families of people who are in acute stages of their illnesses.

Things are so smooth, that I'm not overly concerned when, after several months, Molly tells me she's joined AA. She lets us know that she's been drinking alcohol at these gatherings with her friends and believes that she has a drinking problem. A friend suggested AA and as soon as she went to a meeting, she became convinced that she is an alcoholic.

Peter and I are stumped. Even though we are often asleep when Molly returns home on the weekend evenings from her outings with her new friends, we don't see signs of anything that resembles our notions of alcoholism. She hasn't been so drunk that she's vomited. She doesn't keep drinking during the days. She doesn't have blackouts. However, she should not be drinking any alcohol so I initially choose to see the AA choice as helpful. Since she feels that she wants to drink and she shouldn't, maybe she does have something in common with the people she's meeting. Attending AA also gives her the opportunity to have a good explanation for refusing drinks that people may offer her.

The GED classes haven't provided any new friendships and the AA meetings begin to meet this need. Over the next year, Molly begins attending an increasing number of meetings and has a kind of religious fervour about the work people do there. At least it is a place where people seem to be kind to each other and are tolerant of human frailness. Molly hasn't explained her mental illness to the group and maybe it's good for her to experiment making connections with people without the encumbrance of her diagnosis.

Molly's progress over the year is steady; she's able to do more things by herself. The bus and skytrain rides that her program requires lead to mini-crises in the beginning but become easier to manage. I'm a little disappointed that the staff at VCC make clear that she's not ready for the exams by the end of the year but I completely trust their judgement. It would be destructive for Molly to fail these tests.

They suggest that she spend the fall of 2006 continuing to prepare for exams which she can take in December. The stability of this routine and Molly's lack of a major psychotic relapse for almost four years make it a good time to begin to lower her still extraordinarily high dose of Seroquel. More evidence has been emerging about the dangers of developing diabetes even when there hasn't been a huge weight gain. The Seroquel makes Molly extremely hungry and she has gained about 25 pounds.

Bill develops a plan to very slowly lower Molly's dosage. Usually 400 to 800 mg are considered a maintenance dose. As the dose drops, Molly begins to have more energy. Before, even though she typically went to sleep by 11 pm, she couldn't function in the morning because she was so tired. Fortunately, she only attends GED classes in the afternoon. Her growing ability to function in the morning, on the lowered dose, means that it's easier to arrange the GED exams in early December.

With guidance from VCC's Disability Counselling department and GED staff, I've been able to persuade the Ministry of Education to make important accommodations. Molly will be able to take the five exams over two days instead of during one day and will have more time for each exam. I'd tried, unsuccessfully, to get the exams over three days since one of the documented aspects of her disability is difficulty with sustained focus but I decide not to keep pushing. Now that her dose of Seroquel is 900 mg., Molly is able to arrive for the 9 am start time. Molly believes she has passed the exams and she's right. Some scores are close but the certificate will be mailed to her. We celebrate her remarkable victory.

We visit the main VCC campus several times and Molly starts to feel comfortable being there. She registers for a self-paced Writing Skills 12 course and a Psychology 12 classroom-based course that she can begin in January. Two courses seem like a stretch but the decision is hers and she really wants to try.

In December, even though Molly is mostly doing well, some strange new behaviours develop. People at AA have been discussing all of the triggers in everyday life that can cause relapses. Just being around the alcohol in everyday products like the perfume and mouthwash Molly uses is considered dangerous.

The impact of these comments on her is completely out of proportion to any harm these ingredients pose. She worries that she's developed an addiction to these solvents, as she calls them. At the AA meetings she also hears about the great damage that people have done to their bodies from drinking and she's concerned about her heart. Still, Molly's basic life is so calm that Peter and I decide to leave for a week over Christmas break. Naomi will move home to care for her.

By the end of our week away, things have fallen apart. Molly doesn't think that Naomi really understands her health problems and one night, before Naomi gets home, Molly calls an ambulance to take her to the hospital; she's convinced she's having a heart attack.

Early the next morning as Naomi gets ready for work, she realizes Molly is missing. She calls her cell phone and Molly answers from the hospital where she's had an ECG. Molly interprets this standard response to possible heart attacks as proof that something is wrong. When we return that night, Molly is agitated, angry that Naomi doesn't understand the damage that alcohol has done to her health.

We avoid a confrontation with her, decide to call Bill in the morning, and go to sleep. About midnight she bursts into our room, furious with us for not taking her heart problems seriously. Just as she tells us that an ambulance is on its way, there is banging on the front door. The ambulance attendants are patient with her and she seems calmed by people responding to her emphatic announcement that something's wrong with her.

It's only when one of the attendants takes me aside and asks me what's going on that I start to realize what's been happening. I explain that Molly has schizophrenia but that her illness is well controlled on her medications. The woman asks if there have been any med changes. I start to explain how extremely slowly we've been lowering her dose of Seroquel when I get it.

It's not that the lowering of the dose has been too fast; it's that 900 mg, still an experimentally high dose, isn't supplying what she needs. The ambulance attendants are kind and patient with us all, but even with the explanation have to take her to the hospital for another ECG.

I call the hospital to see what arrangements we can make to pick her up and the duty nurse is miffed that the "Listerine girl" has arrived again. I understand her impatience in an overburdened emergency room. At the same time, I see how Molly was trying to tell herself and us in ways that made sense to her that she has a profound sense that something is terribly wrong with her.

She's right; she just doesn't realize that it's the lowered dose of Seroquel that's the problem. Even so, as usual, she agrees to go back up to 1200 mg and is much less troubled by irrational thoughts over the next few weeks.

The courses are hard for her as is the schedule which is much more demanding. As well, she continues to attend many AA meetings each week and is unable to see that her ideas about the toll alcoholism has taken on her body were part of the confusion of her psychotic illness re-emerging. Things are more strained between us and we don't want to confront her with our understanding of what's been happening.

I'm ready for a vacation by the time Spring Break arrives and one of the support workers moves in for a week. Again, Molly isn't home when we call and we've hardly gotten to talk with her when we return late Sunday afternoon. It's surprising that Molly doesn't arrive home by dinnertime; she likes eating with us. When we call her cell, she says she's with her AA sponsor and they'll be going to a meeting together. She'll be home after that.

Molly always comes home when she says she will or calls to tell us about any changes and we wonder what's happening when she's not home by 9 pm. She's not answering her cell phone. It's fine for her to come home as late as she wants in the evenings but she's always let us know before. By 11 pm, I decide to go to bed; I'm teaching in the morning. I wake at 2 am to hear loud voices in the living room and rush down to find two police officers talking with Peter as he hands them a photo of Molly.

Oh. Now this.

The officers are gentle but insistent. They need to call any of her friends who might know where she is. We supply the numbers and hope all of the support workers and friends with difficult illnesses will forgive us for ruining their night's sleep. It occurs to the younger of the two officers to say one more thing as they wrap up.

He carefully seeks out my eyes to say that things will most likely be just fine; missing people in these kinds of cases almost always quickly turn up. His kindness and empathy for our pain is unexpected; eventually I will learn in a highly publicized report on policing in Vancouver that the shortage of mental health services means that, increasingly, it is police who are the front-line mental health workers.

The police leave and I call the school substitute teacher office; I won't be going to work in the morning.

I think something is somehow going on with the AA sponsor, Jill, and by 4 am she calls us. She says that Molly is safe but she can't tell us where they are; it's confidential. She's calling because the hospital wants to know what prescriptions Molly is on and Jill is coming by cab to pick up the blister pack in which her pills are labelled and organized.

During the phone call, I try to see how much of Molly's illness Jill understands since she's been involved in convincing Molly that her health issues relate to her history of alcoholism. But she is following some protocol and doesn't want to tell me anything except that she will be arriving soon.

Before she gets to our house, I call Vancouver General Hospital Emergency Department and learn that Molly is there. I leave a request for the physician who sees her to call me.

Jill is willing to sit down for a cup of tea when she arrives; she looks relieved that I have the blister pack info ready for her and am ready to support what she's doing. I'm sure that Molly has told her that we don't understand that Molly is an alcoholic and I think Jill is ready to be attacked by parents in denial. She sits on the edge of her chair but responds to my friendly questions.

I become very supportive once she tells me that, after the AA meeting, Molly told her she is planning to hurt herself. Jill thought she should go to the hospital and that it wouldn't be good to answer our calls to her on her cell phone. I try to quickly explain as much as I can about Molly's psychotic disorders and also let her know that Molly has probably drunk less than twenty times in her life. I make sure to let her know that I appreciate the support AA has given her to resist drinking and that alcohol can be dangerous for her.

It's starting to get through to Jill that Molly's situation isn't what she had assumed. Even so, Jill is diligent in telling me, before she gets into the cab that's arrived, how useful Al-Anon can be for family members of alcoholics. She hasn't wanted me to drive her to the hospital; she wants to be in charge of the situation.

I leave a request for the psychiatrist on duty to call me. I hear from him the following morning and explain the history. I'm justifiably worried from Jill's comments that Molly is in danger and I support her admission to VGH's Psychiatric Assessment Unit (PAU) until she can be re-stabilized. I wait through the day for various people to get back to me and about 4 pm hear from the psychiatrist on call that Molly says she's fine so he's going to release her. I know that by now she's missed a complete day's dose of her Seroquel and is in much rougher shape even though she apparently looks fine to him.

Once again, I realize what it means to have the right psychiatrist. We are able to make contact with Bill who immediately calls PAU and requests her admission. I drive over to talk to the admitting psychiatrist. He's been about to end his shift but knows Bill and has stuck around to talk to us.

He asks Molly in front of me if she's fine now and won't hurt herself and she agrees that she's okay. Perhaps this closer look at the unravelling person in front of him or the tone and content of Bill's call has mattered. He agrees to admit her and disappears to do the onerous paperwork.

I try to connect to Molly, telling her what a good idea it had been to come to the hospital when she knew she was in danger. She's coherent enough to tell me that she was given her dose of Zoloft in the morning but not the Seroquel. Maybe the doctors thought they were dealing with a depressed person and the antidepressant was most important. Perhaps the blister pack I sent with the detailed doses labelled by the pharmacist hasn't been seen.

We need the psychiatrist to know that we always stop the Zoloft when she gets agitated and never miss the Seroquel. Being on the reduced 1200 mg dose is what got her into this state; she obviously needs to be back up to 1400 mg. I look for the psychiatrist but he's left; however, an extra dose of Zoloft is waiting for Molly and there's nothing I can say to convince the nurses to delay the dose until we can see another psychiatrist. The staff wants to check her in and it's time for me to leave.

The next morning I begin to use all of the strategies I've been learning to help the situation get under control. I'd recently invited the Manager of PAU to speak at the education sessions I organize for the Vancouver branch of the BCSS. One of the troubling things the audience heard was that it's the policy of the unit to have patients seen by a different psychiatrist each day; this is thought to bring even more opinions into discussions about the patients.

Families were emphatic about how dysfunctional this policy is. The illnesses are complicated and it takes a long time for even one psychiatrist to gain enough understanding of the history and present situation to possibly be able to make a good intervention. Not having a primary psychiatrist at the hospital means that families have a terrible time establishing any communication. We did learn that the best policy is to contact the social worker.

I leave a request for the social worker to call me and let her know that I'm bringing in a one-page summary of

Molly's illness, the doses of medications that she's on, and the list of which medications have been harmful for her. I've learned this strategy from a mom who's a physician and whose son has schizophrenia. Even this simple strategy had never been suggested to the families I know who are eager to reduce the chaos of the hospital. I request an appointment with the psychiatrist who will see Molly.

These strategies work well and by the time I get to the hospital, an appointment has been scheduled for me to briefly see the psychiatrist who has already seen Molly. I also learn from Molly that somehow she still hasn't been given the dose of Seroquel she needs.

The psychiatrist is an expert on co-occurring disorders. We communicate very well; he will be on duty over the next few days and is willing to try to provide some continuity of care. When he brings Molly in, she looks in rough shape and by the end of a short conversation is moving into full blown mania.

She has been aware enough to try to convince the staff that the meds aren't right; the psychiatrist is in complete agreement. With Seroquel about to be restored to 1400 mg, I leave feeling hopeful even though I know Molly's brain chemistry has now launched her on a terrible journey she has tried to resist. Molly spends the next two weeks at PAU and then the UBC Hospital recovering from the med-induced explosion into mania. The experiment during the fall and winter to try to lower Seroquel was necessary but Molly must stay at the unusually high dose of her antipsychotic.

Molly isn't well when she returns home. I'm able to get the assistance of VCCs Disabilities Counsellors to arrange for her to be able to drop the Psychology 12 course even though this deadline is long past. Fortunately, the Writing Skills 12 class is flexible enough that she can just reregister and take it for another term. Molly looks battered by this latest struggle with her illness but the Seroquel is providing a stable foundation to re-enter her life.

Molly's AA sponsor has begun to understand her complicated situation and the comments about all of the damage that her alcoholism has done to her body seem to fade away.

By the fall of 2007, Molly is ready to spend the year applying all the energy she can to mastering English 12 in a self-paced course. She's made great progress in learning to develop and organize her thoughts in an essay and now she's relearning how to read the challenging materials she'd been able to read in elementary school. I become less concerned about the lack of cognitive remediation programs in Vancouver because the thinking skills her focused work at VCC requires are changing her. She's more able to sustain concentration and her ability to participate in a complex conversation keeps growing. All of this translates into increased abilities in many other aspects of her life.

She can also cope with more of the ordinary stresses of daily life. Each term she re-registers at VCC and we sometimes can't avoid dealing with a grumpy office worker. I wonder if this woman has any idea that it takes Molly days to get over her need to humiliate her when we discover that she's forgotten her student card. The woman tells Molly to just hurry and get out her driver's license and snickers when Molly has to explain that she's never had one.

Molly can now register for her courses regardless of which person she has to deal with. She just says that the grumpy woman must have problems of her own.

By January of 2009, Molly is able to take her first college course. VCC offers an *Introduction to Sociology* course which Molly loves until the class begins to focus on the nature of serious mental illnesses. The instructor explains that the pharmaceutical companies, with the help of psychiatrists, have made up a bunch of disorders for which there is no evidence.

Molly raises her hand to tell people that when she's tried to even lower her dose of her antipsychotic, she becomes psychotic. Her instructor assures her this isn't true. When Molly comes home, we go to the National Institute of Mental Health (NIMH) website and print off several articles focusing on the brain scans of people with schizophrenia and on genetic studies. When Molly tries to give these to her instructor before the next class, the instructor glances at them, declares that the NIMH isn't credible, and refuses to read them.

Eventually, we contact the Disabilities Counselling Office which requires medical documentation before offering its students with serious mental illnesses the supports and accommodations they need. We tell them that these comments about mental illnesses not being real pose a genuine risk for students with these disorders; they can easily be persuaded to go off their medications.

Even though Molly really likes sociology, she knows she'll have to pick her future courses carefully. The previous year Simon Fraser University and its Sociology Department held a high profile conference on *Madness, Citizenship and Social Justice*. Perhaps her instructor, like many other grad students in sociology, attended it.

The conference included no presentations by science-based psychiatrists that could have exposed participants to the important idea that most people with bipolar disorder and schizophrenia can get better by taking medications. How ironic that this conference, and the ideas that underlie it, was intended to help people with genuine mental illnesses.

The ideas dominating the conference assert that some people just have emotional problems because of their bad treatment from their families and the societies that marginalize them, and that they are further handicapped by labels that make them seem ill. I know that these ideas can only make the situation of people with schizophrenia and bipolar disorder worse. Why for instance, should they receive any supports or accommodations in their studies if they don't actually have real disorders? Why should they receive disability benefits, supported housing, or any rehabilitation services if they don't have actual illnesses?

The path to recovery is extremely difficult and only more and improved services can increase the likelihood that people with these disorders can rebuild their lives.

151

Not The End

On May 2nd, 2009, Molly speaks on the Stories of Recovery Panel at the 4th annual conference at Vancouver General Hospital on *Family Involvement in the Mental Health System*. Nine years previously she'd just been admitted to Children's Hospital suffering from her first psychotic break.

Molly speaks eloquently and confidently as she describes what she has been through with her illness and how she is rebuilding her life. As the session ends, I watch from a distance as members of several families surround her.

I treasure the richly supportive energy they are extending to her as they congratulate her. I know that their children have been too ill to come to the conference and I recognize the hunger in their faces as they search for anything that can feed their hope.

She has let people know that she was one of the most ill teens in Vancouver and had a grim prognosis. I imagine these harried parents are analyzing the details of her story and trying to see what they might mean for the terrible situations that are crippling their children.

This Family Conference is a major event for both of us. When I returned from NAMI's 2003 Conference, I knew that a conference dedicated to meeting the needs of families could be a success in Vancouver. By 2004, I had drafted a plan for a conference that was endorsed by all of the members of my Mothers Group and their spouses. I took it to a VCMHS staff member involved with family support; he, too, had been thinking that a family conference would be a good idea.

When I joined the VCMHS Family Advisory Committee in 2004, I began taking part in the planning process for our first Family Conference. Working to organize this conference and each of the subsequent family conferences has been one of the most hope-inspiring activities for me during these years.

The conferences are always full and increasing numbers of consumers and mental health staff have begun attending to learn alongside families about the latest research on serious mental illnesses, about the variety of psychosocial rehabilitation programs, and about the stories of family members and consumers who have recovered. There are also stories from the families who are still dealing with very psychotic family members and who wait for the next round of medical breakthroughs.

Molly has told the audience about the four years she spent at VCC where she slowly, with a lot of support from patient teachers, recovered her ability to learn. During the next week she'll begin her new life as a student at Langara College. Molly's life is full; for two years, she has had an amazing boyfriend who understands and accepts her illness.

They love seeing films together, going out to dinner, and going to concerts. Even though he works full-time, they have opportunities to play tennis, golf, and snowboard. They often just eat dinner with us and watch DVDs in our basement. They have fun when they travel and contemplate more trips. They plan a future together.

Molly is very much herself although now her self includes the challenges of managing extremely serious brain disorders. She accepts her illnesses with awe-inspiring equanimity. I had wondered at various points what I should do to assist her in coming to terms with her fate but it's never been necessary. She's worked out her own story and readily details for people the many good things that her life has.

The psychoeducation courses she had at Hamber House, Day Program and through NAMI's BRIDGES Program which has spread across Vancouver's Lower Mainland have given her an extensive understanding of serious mental illnesses; they've also provided ways to construct a new identity that incorporates the development of life-changing illnesses.

Flawed and terribly underfunded as it may be, Vancouver's mental health system provided the necessary ingredients for Molly's miraculous recovery. She spent three years at Hamber House and another year at UBC's Day Program when she was profoundly ill. The programs nurtured her in a variety of ways and kept her safe.

They enabled us to manage to have her continue to live with us. I believe that the support and constant loving attention that she received by living with us made an enormous difference in her eventual recovery. With lots of work and great good fortune, we were able to find and establish relationships with mental health professionals who understood that Molly's best interests were served by collaborating with us and supporting our efforts on her behalf.

This isn't Molly's first public speaking experience. On two previous occasions, she spoke to small intimate gatherings organized by yet more of Vancouver's OTs. Ann Webborn and Tom Heah have created the *Sharing Our Success Stories* series which regularly profiles the recoveries and achievements of a wide variety of Vancouver's consumers. The series is filmed and at these conferences the table set up to distribute the DVD's of these events always does a lively business. I know well the desperation of families looking for any evidence that people can get better from the worst of these illnesses.

Before each of these presentations, Molly met with Ann Webborn who skilfully helps people develop the stories they are going to tell and helps provide the confidence they need to do public speaking, an undertaking most people find stressful. In doing public speaking, Molly has begun to realize, in a deeper way, that her survival and the redevelopment of the skills most people take for granted are actually extraordinary accomplishments.

As the nurse at Children's Hospital inappropriately urged me to do nine years ago, I am letting go. Though still disabled in significant ways, Molly is able to guide her own life.

But if I had let go during these past nine years, just as would have happened on that long-ago dock on Gabriola Island, Molly could have drowned. I imagine many parents I know, mostly mothers, throwing themselves down on the docks they had mistakenly trusted. They are holding on as

155

tightly as they can and their head-injured sons and daughters linger just below the surface; the dangerous black water is ready to swallow them up. I hear them shouting for help for their children and themselves but I'm not sure if people on the boats nearby understand their screams.

Useful Websites

The following websites provide help in learning about such topics as:

- serious mental illnesses,
- the medications used to treat them,
- psychoeducation and supports for consumers and families
- recent research,
- legal issues,
- useful books,
- stories of people who have recovered to varying degrees or in some tragic cases, not at all, from these disorders.

www.nami.org
NAMI (which formerly stood for the National Alliance for the Mentally Ill) is the largest advocacy group in the world for people with mental illnesses and their families. Canadians have a lot to learn from the successful advocacy strategies that NAMI helps people develop.

www.mentalhealth.com
Developed by Dr. Phil Long, a deeply respected Vancouver psychiatrist, this lively website is maintained by consumers hired privately by Dr. Long.

www.schizophrenia.com
This comprehensive website includes blogs from consumers and family members.

www.treatmentadvocacy.org and www.cfact.ca
These websites help educate people on the legal issues involved in working towards timely treatment for people with severe psychiatric illnesses. Families often want to work towards a system that protects people's right to be well rather than the right to be ill. Currently this is difficult both in Canada and the US.

www.mentalhealthcommission.ca
The Mental Health Commission of Canada, after studying mental health policies in various countries, is working to develop a national mental health strategy.

www.nimh.nih.gov
The US National Institute of Mental Health is the largest research organization in the world working towards the prevention and cure of mental illnesses.

www.cprf.ca
The Canadian Psychiatric Research Foundation has funded over 400 research projects in universities and teaching hospitals across the country.

www.stanleyresearch.org
The Stanley Medical Research Institute is the largest private, non-profit research organization in the world focused on the treatment and causes of schizophrenia and bipolar disorder.

www.schizophrenia.ca
The website of the Schizophrenia Society of Canada offers
a variety of resources.

www.cmha.ca
The Canadian Mental Health Association has information
on psychiatric problems and on resources useful to families.

Recommended Books

Adamec, Christine. (1996). *How to Live with a Mentally Ill Person: A Handbook of Day-to-Day Strategies*. Toronto: John Wiley & Sons

Backlar, Patricia. (1994). *The Family Face of Schizophrenia*. New York: Penguin Putnam Inc.

Campbell, Bebe Moore. (2005) *72 Hour Hold*. New York: Alfred A. Knopf

Jamison, Kay. (1995). *An Unquiet Mind: a Memoir of Moods and Madness*. New York: Vintage

Karp, David. (2001). *The Burden of Sympathy: How Families Cope with Mental Illness*. New York: Oxford University Press

Lefley, Harriet. (1996). *Family Caregiving in Mental Illness*. Thousand Oaks: Sage

Marsh, Diane and Dickens, Rex. (1997). *How to Cope with Mental Illness in Your Family: A Self-Care Guide for Siblings, Offspring, and Parents*. New York: Tarcher Putnam

Mondimore, Francis. (1999). *Bipolar Disorder: A Guide for Patients and Families*. Baltimore: Johns Hopkins University Press

Mueser, Kim and Gingerich, Susan. (1994). *Coping with Schizophrenia: A Guide for Families*. Oakland: New Harbinger

Park, Clara Claiborne.(1995) *The Siege: A Family's Journey into the World of an Autistic Child.* New York: Little, Brown and Company

Paris, Joel. (2005). *The Fall of an Icon: Psychoanalysis and Academic Psychiatry.* Toronto: University of Toronto Press

Ross, Marvin. (2008). *Schizophrenia: Medicine's Mystery, Society's Shame.* Dundas: Bridgeross

Schwartz, Jeffrey. (1996). *Brainlock: Free Yourself from Obsessive-Compulsive Behavior.* New York: HarperCollins

Shorter, Edward. (1997). *A History of Psychiatry: From the Era of the Asylum to the Age of Prozac.* Toronto: John Wiley & Sons

Simmie, Scott and Nunes, Julie. (2001). *The Last Taboo: A Survival Guide to Mental Health Care in Canada.* Toronto: McClelland & Stewart Ltd.

Torrey, E Fuller. (1992). *Freudian Fraud: The Malignant Effect of Freud's Theory on American Thought and Culture.* New York: HarperCollins

Torrey, E. Fuller. (2006). *Surviving Schizophrenia: A Manual for Families, Patients, and Providers* (5th edition). New York: HarperCollins

Wasow, Mona. (2000). *The Skipping Stone: Ripple Effects of Mental Illness on the Family.* Palo Alto: Science and Behaviour Books, Inc.

Glossary of Terms

Antipsychotic medications – are used to treat the symptoms of psychosis such as those found in schizophrenia. The first group of these drugs were discovered in the 1950s and are referred to as typical. **Haldol** (haloperidol) is the best known of these but there are others such as **Chlorpromazine** and **Fluphenazine**. While effective, these drugs have some very serious **extrapyramidal** side effects such as jerky, involuntary motions of the head, neck, arms, body, or eyes. This is known as **Tardive Dyskinesia.**

The recent antipsychotics are known as atypical because their mode of action is different and they are not supposed to cause the extrapyramidal side effects so common with the first generation of drugs. These include **Clozapine, Zyprexa, Risperidone, Seroquel, Geodon/Zeldox, Abilify,** and **Invega.**

Benzodiazepines – such as **Librium, Valium, Ativan, Clonazepam** and others are very effective anti-anxiety medications and are used for a wide variety of conditions ranging from panic attacks to muscle spasms. They are very highly addictive.

Bipolar disorder – was formerly called manic depression and is characterized by episodes of depression alternating with euphoric or dysphoric manic states. The symptoms of bipolar disorder are complex and often affect an individual's daily functioning and interpersonal relationships.

Cognitive Behavioural Therapy (CBT) – refers to a range of techniques that grew out of behavioural psychology and focuses on helping people master strategies to change unwanted thoughts and behaviours

Depression characterized by a greater intensity and duration and by more severe symptoms and functional disabilities than is normal.

Obsessive compulsive disorder (OCD) - the sufferer experiences repeated obsessions and/or compulsions that interfere with the person's ability to function socially, occupationally, or educationally, either as a result of the amount of time that is consumed by the symptoms or the marked fear or other distress suffered by the person.

Schizophrenia – a chronic, severe, and disabling brain disorder that has affected people throughout history. About 1 percent of people have this illness. It is characterized by three broad sets of symptoms – positive such as hallucinations and delusions; negative such as lack of motivation and affect and, thirdly, cognitive loss. Its onset is typically ages 16-30

Schizoaffective disorder – is a disease that has features of both schizophrenia and a mood disorder such as bipolar disorder or severe depression.

Treatment for Bipolar Disorder – The standard treatment is **Lithium** but in the past few years, a number of the drugs used to treat epilepsy such as **Valproate (Depakote)** and **Carbamezapine (Tegretol)** have been used to stabilize mood. Some of the atypical antipsychotics have also been approved by regulatory agencies to treat bipolar disorder.

Treatment for Depression – The most commonly prescribed drugs for this condition are those that are known as selective serotonin reuptake inhibitors or SSRI's. The first drug in this category was **Prozac** but there are many others such as **Paxil** and **Zoloft**. This class of drugs are also approved for the treatment of **anxiety disorders** and **OCD**

An older class of anti-depressants are called **tricyclic antidepressants (TCA's)**. They were first developed in the 1950s but they are still sometimes used today for those who do not respond to the newer drugs. There are about 10 different ones but the most commonly recognized is **Elavil**. They are used to treat depression and many of the other psychiatric diseases.

Biography

Susan has written numerous articles on topics related to serious mental illnesses for a variety of Canadian publications including *The Globe and Mail*, the *Vancouver Province*, and the online journal *The Tyee*.

She continues to participate in public speaking at events large and small about the experiences of families dealing with serious mental illnesses.

She is currently vice-chair of the Family Advisory Committee (FAC) of Vancouver Coastal Mental Health Services (VCMHS). Since 2005, she has been involved in organizing an annual Family Conference co-sponsored by the FAC, VCMHS, the BCSS, and the Mood Disorder Association of BC.

A Past-President of the Vancouver/Richmond Branch of the British Columbia Schizophrenia Society (BCSS), she received, in 2005, an award from the BCSS in recognition of her "outstanding service and dedication to alleviate the suffering caused by schizophrenia and other serious mental illnesses"

She created and produced, in partnership with the Schizophrenia Society of Canada, the BCSS, and Playwrights Theatre Centre (PTC) in Vancouver, the *This Is a Spoon* one-act play writing contest for scripts dealing with schizophrenia. This national contest culminated in June, 2003, in two evenings of sold-out performances of professionally staged readings at PTC of the winning script.

Susan received a BA from Swarthmore College and an MA from UCLA. She has taught drama and English at Windermere Secondary School in Vancouver for almost twenty years.

Susan can be contacted through the publisher for interviews and personal appearances.

LaVergne, TN USA
13 October 2010
200662LV00001B/43/P